Daughters *of* Jerusalem

The title has many meanings.
Daughter was a term used to describe
the various quadrants of the city of
Jerusalem. Luke may be calling out to
Jerusalem as a city or to all the women
who have followed the ancient
religion of the Jews. It is both a
political and an endearing term.

Daughters _of_ Jerusalem

"Daughters of Jerusalem,
do not weep
for me."

Luke 23:28

Marla J. Selvidge

Foreword by Willard M. Swartley

HERALD PRESS
Scottdale, Pennsylvania
Kitchener, Ontario
1987

Library of Congress Cataloging-in-Publication Data

Selvidge, Marla J., 1948-
  Daughters of Jerusalem.

  Bibliography: p.
  Includes index.
  1. Women—Biblical teaching.   2. Women in the Bible.
3. Bible. N.T. Gospels—Criticism, Redaction.
I. Title.
BS2545.W65S45   1987   226'.083054   87-7437
ISBN 0-8361-3440-0 (pbk.)

DAUGHTERS OF JERUSALEM
Copyright © 1987 by Herald Press, Scottdale, Pa. 15683-1999
      Published simultaneously in Canada by Herald Press,
      Kitchener, Ont. N2G 4M5. All rights reserved.
Library of Congress Card Catalog Number: 87-7437
International Standard Book Number: 0-8361-3440-0
Printed in the United States of America
Cover art by Phyllis Magal
Design by Gwen M. Stamm

87 88 89 90 91 92 93 94 10 9 8 7 6 5 4 3 2 1

With love and appreciation
to my mother,
Mary M. Gilreath-Selvidge,
who is not afraid to challenge the system.
Her hard work, strength, and love is the
foundation of
our family.

In memory
of my father,
William Lester 'Les' Selvidge,
who put a paintbrush,
a hoe, and a lawnmower
in my hands
while arguing
politics,
religion,
and life.

Acknowledgement

Many thanks to Angie Janulis who meticulously read this manuscript, checked my references, and encouraged me throughout the entire project.

Contents

Foreword

During the last two decades much literature has appeared on the role of women in the Bible. Within the New Testament much of this has focused on the Pauline texts with attempts to correlate two diverse strands of thought—that of women freely participating in a variety of early church ministries (Rom. 16:1-7; 1 Cor. 11:1-16; Phil. 4:2-3) and that of restrictions placed upon women (1 Cor. 14:34-35; 1 Tim. 2:11-12). Jesus' relation to and teaching about women has been cited in support of the new freedom and worth for women.

Only in a few instances has the larger interpretive issue of the standpoint of the Gospels—written after Paul's letters—emerged for careful scrutiny. When the Pauline restrictive texts are assigned to a post-Pauline authorship and date, it becomes all the more crucial to pay adequate attention to the standpoint of the Gospels on this matter. This must be done in order to arrive at a proper assessment of the Christian church's understanding of the place and ministry of women in the church in the last third of the first century.

Elisabeth Schüssler Fiorenza's ground-breaking *In Memory of Her* illustrates well the failure in this regard. The overall portrait of first-century Christianity is one of gradual decline for the freedom and service of women in the church. Her brief treatment of the Gospels at the end of her book shows her own awareness that their testimony counts, but her failure to adequately incorporate that testimony into her overall reconstruction and portrait is typical of research of the last several decades.

In light of the history of research on this issue, Marla Selvidge's study makes a significant contribution. Selvidge's goal is to understand how women are portrayed in the synoptic Gospels. This effort is the first step toward the larger task of understanding the overall picture of the place of women in the church during the first century.

What Selvidge does well—and more convincingly for Mark and Luke than for Matthew—is to show that each of these Gospels puts women in positive roles in the Gospel narratives. She understands this to reflect the roles that women carried as a result of the strains, chaos, and social disintegration caused by the A.D. 66-70 wars. Amid the crises of these times women emerged in roles of service, leadership, and familial commitment in such a way as to influence the portrait in the Gospel stories.

On this point Selvidge gives too much credit to the wars. She rightly connects these emphases also to Jesus' own life and teaching. But more should be made of this and of other types of needs and developments in the early churches as well.

Selvidge also seeks to connect her research on the Gospels with the challenges facing women today. This challenge, as she sees it, is for women to contribute to present needs and crises in a variety of ways. Leadership? Yes. But also compassionate service which women know well how to do. They should continue to give, but recognize also their limits. The overall goal is the health and goodness of the society (home and church) of which they are a part.

Of the many good contributions which this book makes, its strongest, in my judgment, is the sensitive and vital descriptions of the women portrayed in the Gospels. Her description of the woman with a hemorrhage in Mark 5:24-33 enables us to see many new dimensions in both the strength of this woman and in the significance of this story in the Gospel tradition. The same can be said for her portrait of Jesus' mother Mary in Luke, the woman of Bethany who anointed Jesus for burial, and the women who served and followed Jesus.

I recommend this book not because I agree with all its assumptions about the factors influencing the Gospel portraits, but because it shows us clearly that any attempt to reconstruct the role of women in the early church must take into account the Gospels and their testimony of good news for women and men today.

—Willard M. Swartley
Professor of New Testament
Associated Mennonite Biblical Seminaries

Daughters
of
Jerusalem

Introduction

The Christian world has discovered woman. The market is flooded with books about what it means to be a woman and a Christian today. This discovery and trend has led to a division between radical feminists and traditionalists.

Radical feminists abandon the biblical traditions claiming that they see only male writers, male values, and a male-worldview. God is male. The biblical view of woman does not fit into their lifestyles or their ambitions for life. They claim freedoms of vocation for all women. Traditionalists staunchly uphold the view about women that fits into a male-dominated world. They militantly argue for the right to serve, to raise their children, to stay home, and to become the support structures for the home.

Neither of these approaches facilitates peace between women or men. And neither is solely advocated by the gospel writers. Matthew, Mark, and Luke wrote about a diversity of women and a diversity of lifestyles. By studying their documents, we realize that Christianity welcomes all types of women with all types of talents. None is preferred over the other. All must be who they are and use their talents in order for life to be everything it can be.

Since the feminist explosion of the late 1960s, the topic of woman has headlined many writings on the gospels. At first their questions centered on Jesus' view of women.[1] Their answers became an apology for women's liberation in the church and society.[2] As more critical investigative tools were employed, their questions began to center not on Jesus' view of woman, but on understanding how the early church pictured woman.[3] The next step is already taking place. People are beginning to discover the individual thoughts of the gospel writers.

The gospels were written as proclamation, as story. In a very real way they reflect the mind of at least three individuals that lived during the first century C.E. The views of these people seem to be "feminist." Their inclusive stance and respect for all persons is a goal that we of the twentieth century are still attempting to achieve.

Sexism and racism are vital issues. These problems were no less important during the war years of the first and second century C.E. According to the Synoptics, women not only overcome social oppression; they turn physical pain and grief into a celebration. In spite of harassment due to an illegitimate pregnancy, debilitating physical pain and illness, sexist and racist attitudes toward foreigners—and in spite of past histories that found some in professions that were questionable by the pious of society—women emerge triumphant. Their presence is felt in all of the stories from the beginning of Jesus' life until the end. They never give up nor do they turn their backs on Jesus. They, too, may have paid the ultimate price for service.

Mark, Matthew, and Luke tell stories about women who were part of the rebuilding of a society and a religious heritage. Their stories bring structure into a chaotic world of economic desolation. The evangelists seek to link the readers with the past and then give them hope for a better future. In capturing the meaning of Jesus for their communities, they place women at the center.

These stories seem to be timeless. For over two thousand years, their messages have rung true to people all over the earth. The Bible is a book about life—about people who searched and found, and others who became frustrated along the way. Its mysteries, sometimes unlocked, usually give way to more unanswerable questions.

Over the centuries fascinated inquirers used their imagination to unlock the meanings of texts within the Bible. Some of the earliest interpreters of the New Testament concluded that most of the stories should be interpreted in an allegorical or symbolic way.[4] For instance, the story about the woman with a flow of blood for twelve years became a story about how the Gentile church was cleansed.[5] Ambrose said it was a story about corruption in the church.

> The likeness of thy church is that woman who went behind and touched the hem of thy garment saying within herself, "If I do but touch his garment I shall be whole." So the church confesses her wounds but desires to be healed.[6]

Years before the invention of the printing press, manuscripts of the Bible were accessible to only a few. Educated priests and affluent lay persons benefited most from the direct use of handwritten copies of the New

Testament. The average person (if at mass on Sunday) could hear the ancient words and see the stories of the book in the stained-glass windows. But that person would never become personally involved in unlocking the meanings of parables or puzzling miracle stories. The opened book resting upon the table near the altar in front of the church would always contain divine, mysterious, and distant words.

A remarkable change has occurred in biblical studies. The Bible is accessible to almost everyone. It has been translated into all major languages. Even blind and deaf people have versions to read and hear. People attending church today are well-educated in world affairs and history. They are ready for an intellectual challenge. Their curiosity about the ancient texts often unearths unanswerable questions.[7] They have discovered that upon studying the same passage, each person will have a different view of the text.

Often, if people who study the Bible are honest with themselves, they will see that they are bringing their own ideas to the text. In a sense, they view the Bible through their own glasses colored with their own particular perceptions about life. Each question that they pose begins to probe the pages of the Bible for an answer. Sometimes the biblical writers address the question and at other times they are silent.

Questioning is at the heart of biblical scholarship. As students question the text, a sort of "conversation" or "dialogue" emerges. Conversing with the writers of the biblical stories may be like conversing with friends. Sometimes you understand them and sometimes you do not. Your understanding depends upon many variables. Were you listening to everything your friend said? Have you taken your friend's words out of context? Perhaps your friend used words that were unfamiliar to you? What was your state of mind when you were talking with your friend? Were you asking unanswerable questions?

Conversing with the Bible is not a passive activity. Students' involvement in the conversation must be very active in order to understand the relevancy of the texts for people today and in the future. Translations of these texts may change as we discover older manuscripts or more historical information. The ancient biblical writers used different languages. The most educated translators must make decisions based upon their own views of the text. When students begin a conversation with the Bible they must realize that they are speaking with people who lived thousands of years ago and spoke languages like Greek, Aramaic, and Hebrew. These people now speak through an interpreter who may make a mistake or misunderstand the meaning of a sentence or word, or fail to give alternative interpretations of the text for the benefit of the readers.

During the last two centuries several ways of questioning or conversing with the Bible have been named and developed into methodologies of study. For instance, students discovered that there were thousands of manuscripts and fragments of manuscripts of the New Testament.[8] Upon examining these diverse works, they discovered that they differed with each other. Sometimes while comparing verses they would find that words were left out, added, spelled incorrectly, or changed by the person who handcopied the work. For example, in the best and oldest manuscripts, the Gospel of Mark ends with 16:8. In most Bibles, the translators will note that there are several possible endings to Mark.[9] In an effort to determine which of the readings of the texts was the oldest and most likely text to have been originally composed, students began to develop a way of solving this problem. They termed this methodology textual criticism.[10]

Others discovered that the writers of the gospels were using contemporary literary forms found in many ancient literatures. They realized that the meaning of a passage is influenced by the form in which it is written. For instance, the punchline of a joke will have a different meaning than a transcript of an event. The punchline is meant to be ironical, sarcastic, or funny. The transcript aims at accuracy. The gospel writers were not transcribers. They were teachers and preachers who attempted to communicate important theological, social, and personal ideas about Jesus and their world.

Two German students, Martin Dibelius and Rudolph Bultmann, earlier in this century devised outlines whereby the readers of the gospels would be able to recognize certain forms.[11] One of the most widely used forms of writing in the gospels was the miracle story. But not every miracle story is about the same kind of miracle. They classified these miracles into types. There are exorcisms, general healings, raisings from the dead, and nature miracles.[12] Generally miracle stories contained these items:

1. Length of sickness
2. Dreadful or dangerous character of the disease
3. Ineffective treatment of physicians
4. Doubt and contemptuous treatment of the healer[13]

Dibelius and Bultmann suggested that the writers of the gospels did indeed use many contemporary literary forms to communicate their messages about Jesus and their communities. In addition to miracle stories, they used narratives, parables, controversy sayings, genealogies, and much, much more.[14]

As more and more people began to read and study the Bible, they began to see distinct differences and similarities in the stories found in the gospels. They began to ask questions: If all of the gospel writers were eyewitnesses, then why are so many sentences similar in all three gospels? Why does Matthew seem to incorporate so much of Mark? Why were three similar gospels included in the Bible?

Students of the Bible explored these questions about the differences and similarities of the gospels and began to develop a host of theories as to the origins of the Synoptics—Matthew, Mark, and Luke. One very popular theory is the Four Document Hypothesis.[15]

Several researchers suggested that Matthew and Luke used a variety of different sources during the writing and editing of each of their gospels.[16] When Matthew wrote the gospel, the writer had knowledge of the Gospel of Mark, ancient birth and resurrection stories, and a document that preserved "sayings of Jesus." This last document is termed "Q" for "sayings source" *(Quelle)*. With knowledge of these accounts and documents about Jesus, Matthew put together a gospel for Matthew's own special community. Matthew attempted to meet this community's needs by telling them stories about Jesus.

In the same vein, Luke was a researcher, an interviewer—a compiler of stories, who had access to differing traditions about the birth and resurrection of Jesus. Luke admits that the goal of the Gospel of Luke was to write a connected narrative.

Inasmuch as many have undertaken to compile a narrative of the things which have been accomplished among us, just as they were delivered to us by those who from the beginning were eyewitnesses and ministers of the word, it seemed good to me also, having followed all things closely for some time past, to write an orderly account for you, most excellent Theophilus, that you may know the truth concerning the things of which you have been informed.

(Luke 1:1-4, RSV)

Luke used at least as many sources as Matthew. Luke had knowledge of Mark, "Q," and special sources that provided the writer with stories about John the Baptist's birth, Mary's views on the birth and childhood of Jesus, and a host of parables. All of the gospels used the Hebrew and Greek versions of Scripture (the Old Testament) as they reflected upon the meaning and message of Jesus.

Other students of the Bible disagree with the above theory. Many suggest that Matthew was written first and that the material common with Luke is there because Luke relied heavily on Matthew. They also hold that Mark is only an abridged version of Matthew.[17]

No one will ever know the exact literary route the gospels took in the ancient world. We do know that all of the gospel writers were interested in oral and written traditions about Jesus. Similarly they portray a messiah that dies on the cross. Yet they also view Jesus differently. By including their own emphases and material about Jesus, they meet the needs of their own communities in a special way. For instance, Luke sees Jesus as a social activist. Mary sighs a prophecy concerning her child, Jesus,

For behold, henceforth all generations will call me blessed; for he who is mighty has done great things for me, and holy is his name.

And his mercy is on those who fear him from generation to generation.

He has shown strength with his arm, he has scattered the proud in the imagination of their hearts, he has put down the mighty from their thrones, and exalted those of low degree; he has filled the hungry with good things, and the rich he has sent empty away.
(Luke 1:48-53, RSV)

Matthew, schooled in the traditions of the Jews, reminds the audience that Jesus was predicted by the ancient writers. Over and over again the phrase "that it might be fulfilled" is used by Matthew (1:22-23; 2:5-6; 2:15, 2:17-18; 2:23; 4:14-16; 8:17; 12:17-21; 13:35; 21:4-5; 27:9-10).[18] For this writer, Jesus was the New Moses. His authority is greater than Moses'! In the Sermon on the Mount, Jesus verbally reinterprets the teachings said to have been given to the Israelites through Moses. "Do not suppose that I have come to abolish the Law and the prophets; I did not come to abolish, but to complete" (Matt. 5:17, NEB), is the beginning of a new way of life for those who would listen to Jesus.

Mark's gospel tells stories about a different kind of messiah. Jesus is primarily a miracle worker. Mark chooses to include active material in the story about Jesus. Most of the first eight chapters of Mark deal with healings of Jesus. And the ending of Mark has puzzled people for centuries.

The women who witnessed the empty tomb "said nothing to anybody, for they were afraid" (Mark 16:8, NEB).

The process whereby we have identified some of the gospel writer's individual views of Jesus is termed Redaction Criticism.[19] A redactor is an editor. By comparing stories or concentrating upon material that is found only in one of the gospels, a student will begin to see that the writers of the gospels edited the stories they collected. Their editing reveals distinctive views on many subjects.

In researching women in the Synoptics, I began the conversation by asking each writer about his views on women. I examined every story about a woman mentioned in each gospel. Since it is impossible to consider every literary theory about the origins of the gospels, I accepted the traditional theory that Mark was written first and that Matthew and Luke used Mark as a source. I analyzed how Matthew and Luke made use of the material in Mark and I asked questions about why they chose to tell the stories as they did and how their shaping of the stories fit into their overall view of women. I also analyzed the stories found only in one of the gospels. For instance, Mark is the only gospel with the question about the fearful women in 16:8. Matthew adds women to the genealogy in the first chapter. Luke tells the story of Jesus' birth from Mary's point of view (Luke 1—2).

While this study is primarily literary, often I will seek out explanations for texts by turning to the time period in which the gospels were written. Strictly speaking this is not a pure redaction criticism. The reason that I searched elsewhere for answers to questions in the text is that every piece of literature is influenced by the times in which it was written. To divorce a work from its cultural heritage is to lose valuable clues regarding its intended message.

Over the past fifteen years I have consistently integrated the question about women and the Bible into my research, my writing, and my teaching. This book reflects that lengthy conversation with all three writers.

1

MARK'S STORY

Daughter as Leader

*"My daughter, your faith has cured you.
Go in peace, free for ever from this
trouble." (Mark 5:34, NEB)*

Introduction

Whoever reads the Gospel of Mark for the first time becomes spellbound by the miracle worker, Jesus. He is a
servant of God who demands complete allegiance from his
followers (8:34). For Mark this servant of God has no personal past, only a public present and a future. Jesus' homelife and personal relationships are not important to this
writer who waits at the edge.[1] Time is suspended as the
writer waits for Jesus to return somewhere in northern
Palestine, to Galilee (Mark 16:7).

Mark began writing this gospel during or after the
destruction of Jerusalem. The city seems to be in ruins.

> You see these great buildings? Not one stone will be
> left upon another; all will be thrown down.
>
> (Mark 13:2, NEB)

Like this magnificent city, the Jewish hierarchy—the power structure of Jerusalem—also lay in ruins. Out of the dust, people were gathering to fight for their lives and to grapple with a new type of communal existence based upon stories about the miracle worker, Jesus. These people needed a miracle. Mark offers them a hopeful future undergirded with the demands of a present sacrificial lifestyle.

Although many scholars believe Mark to be the oldest surviving canonical gospel, it has never been as popular as the Gospel of Matthew. Nor has it been studied as much as the Gospel of Luke.[2] The oldest surviving commentary on Mark is from the seventh century A.D.—four hundred years after commentaries on Matthew and Luke had been written and rewritten.[3]

Mark's lack of popularity could be due to its fragmented account about Jesus which preserves no stories about Jesus' birth and resurrection. These traditions became the basis for important creedal statements about the virgin birth, bodily resurrection, and ascension of Jesus.[4] Some claim that Mark did preserve a resurrection appearance story at the end of Mark 16:8. It was lost, discarded, or destroyed.[5] Ancient manuscripts contain a variety of endings for Mark, but none has received consensus as part of Mark's original gospel.

Mark's gospel may also have been neglected because of its controversial stance toward the twelve. Their leadership capabilities and allegiance are questioned. In Mark they do not intuitively perceive nor intellectually understand the identity and mission of Jesus. Ironically a host of other people emerge as those most willing to follow and serve Jesus. Among those people Mark highlights women. They are viewed as the strength of the community as stories are told about lives as faith-healers and spokespersons for the future.

The Twelve as Failures

If we read the Gospel of Mark with a sensitive eye, we find something very startling. Although the twelve are selected as personal assistants of Jesus, they never actually carry out his teachings. They are not portrayed as actually living or practicing Jesus' ideals.[6] They do not risk their lives. They do not deny themselves, nor do they give up all of their possessions. They follow, but their journey does not take them down every road that Jesus takes. Their "front-line" service is momentary and minimal in the Gospel of Mark.

Having left their homes, they briefly engage in an itinerate healing campaign where they anoint, heal the sick, and cast out demons (Mark 6:13). These activities are not featured in Mark as complete stories. In only one story are some of the twelve faced with using their "powers." They fail. They could not heal the boy possessed by a demonic spirit (Mark 9:18).

Theodore J. Weeden, like many others, discusses the failure of the twelve in Mark.[7] The twelve are disciples but they are not the only disciples. *Disciple* seems to be a general term for any follower in Mark.[8] Elizabeth Struthers Malbon suggests that the twelve mirror all people of all time that read this gospel. All fail like the twelve.[9] Yet a closer study of Mark reveals that some fail, others do not.

A brief survey of the gospel surfaces some surprising evidence. Who turned Jesus over to the authorities? Who abandoned Jesus at the moment of his arrest? Who stayed with and near Jesus during his entire ordeal? Who understood the meaning of self-denial and service? The following pages will answer these questions as the failure of the twelve is outlined and the success of others is considered.

James and John were followers of Jesus. They were handpicked. They were part of the inner circle. They should have known and understood Jesus and his teachings better than anyone else. Yet they are the ones who demonstrate most what it means to be self-seeking and self-centered.

> James and John, the sons of Zebedee, approached him and said, "Master, we should like you to do us a favour." "What is it you want me to do?" he asked. They answered, "Grant us the right to sit in state with you, one at your right and the other at your left."
> (Mark 10:35-38, NEB)

> When the other ten heard this, they were indignant with James and John.   (Mark 10:41, NEB)

This story may be a recollection or a literary creation of the writer about a militant side of the twelve. Perhaps some of Jesus' followers thought that he had intentions of overthrowing the Roman emperor. Two of the twelve see Jesus as a potential ruler or very powerful person. Their concern is only for themselves.

Historically the Jews had survived domination and oppression by the Egyptians, Assyrians, Babylonians, Persians, Greeks, Ptolemies, Seleucids, and their own liberal party known as the Maccabees. Now they were living under the Romans and waiting anxiously for the day when they would be self-governing again.[10] James and John wanted to know if they were going to have any power in Jesus' new regime.

Jesus was outraged by their lack of understanding. He had no intention of being a dictator nor of running a world-wide government. His rule, if you can call it a rule, was one of service to humanity. Jesus called for a reversal in thinking (Mark 10:44). People who care about others do not create personal empires. Empires are for people who want to control others. Controlling and thus oppressing people is not the way of Jesus.

> "You know that in the world the recognized rulers lord it over their subjects, and their great men make them feel the weight of authority. That is not the way with you; among you, whoever wants to be great must be your servant, and whoever wants to be first must be the willing slave of all."
>
> (Mark 10:42-44, NEB)

Serving included death for Jesus; it might include death for others (Mark 10:38, 45).

The twelve never grasp these ideals. Often Jesus takes them aside and personally explains parables about his kingdom and his rule (Mark 7:7). They do not seem to listen nor do they understand what it means to "follow" Jesus. In the beginning of Mark's gospel the writer seems to praise James and John for following Jesus.

> Leaving their father Zebedee in the boat with the hired men, they went off to follow him.
>
> (Mark 1:20, NEB)

These two leave their families without good-byes or promises of return. This personal loss of their sons or cousins is never explored by the writer. Nor does Mark's story include a section about the financial state of the Zebedee family or business. What would have happened to their business as a result of the loss of two healthy sons? Mark may suggest that their following was far from total.

> Then the disciples all deserted him and ran away.
> (Mark 14:50, NEB; see also 14:32)

They who so quickly left their family business and responsibilities now abandon their responsibilities again. Their following was only temporary and Mark hints that they followed Jesus for all the wrong reasons.

The inner circle of Peter, James, and John continues to fail Jesus. Peter complains about leaving so much behind (Mark 10:28) and is unable to accept Jesus' imminent death (Mark 8:31). He alone recognizes Jesus' identity as Messiah, but he also misinterprets the meaning of that title. Jesus reprimands Peter. "Away with you, Satan," he said; "you think as men think, not as God thinks" (Mark 8:33, NEB).

Peter especially seems to fail in the Gospel of Mark. Peter totally abandons Jesus. Peter follows Jesus at a distance. As he watches, he protects himself by denying his relationship with Jesus. In self-defense, Peter "broke out into curses" (Mark 14:71, NEB). This phrase "broke out into curses" can be translated "cursed himself" or "cursed" something or someone else. Mark may be implying that Peter actually "anathematized" or "cursed" Jesus (i.e., condemned him to hell).[11] Peter totally denies Jesus but

Jesus does not forget Peter. Mark's story ends with a hopeful note. The women are told to "go, tell his disciples and Peter" (Mark 16:7).[12] So there is hope for Peter.

This total abandonment of Jesus by the inner circle and the twelve is placed next to stories about other people who do not abandon Jesus. Uppermost on the list of people who remain loyal to Jesus are the women. Although women do not have large speaking roles in the narratives, they are always present in the crowds and on the sidelines. Donald Michie and David Rhoades in their book, *Mark as Story*, includes them among the "little people." To these people, say Michie and Rhoades, the community must look for role models and guidance.[13] The traditions preserved about women create a story about successful followers of Jesus. These woman-traditions become a source of inspiration for both sexes during the troubled times of the first century.

Sexual Segregation and the Hemorrhaging Woman

For Mark the miracle story about the hemorrhaging woman is really a story about people who suffer because of rigid religious ideals or beliefs. Her problem was long-term and very personal. It separated her from her family, friends, and a potential physical relationship with a man.

And there was a woman who had had a flow of blood for twelve years, and who had suffered much under many physicians, and had spent all that she had, and was no better but rather grew worse. She had heard the reports about Jesus, and came up behind him in the crowd and touched his garment. For she said, "If I touch even his garments, I shall be made well." And immediately the hemorrhage ceased; and she felt in her body that she was healed of her disease. And Jesus, perceiving in himself that power had gone forth from him, immediately turned about in the crowd, and said, "Who touched my garments?" And his disciples said to him, "You see the crowd pressing around you, and yet you say, 'Who touched me?'" And he looked around to see who had done it. But the woman, knowing what had been done to her, came in fear and trembling and fell down before him, and told him the whole truth. And he said to her, "Daughter, your faith has made you well; go in peace, and be healed of your disease."   (Mark 5:25-34, RSV)

This story is about a desperately alienated woman. It is also a story about the social alienation that many people may have felt who attempted to live according to the purity laws within traditional Judaism.

She had a "hemorrhage" or "flow of blood." In researching this term throughout Greek literature, I found both of these terms used only by the writers of Leviticus.[14] The Greek translation of the Hebrew Scriptures (Old Testament) only used these terms when detailing laws concerning a woman during her menstrual cycle. This story is about a woman who had a chronic gynecological problem. Mark may have preserved this story because it illustrated a woman's predicament in a society that segregated her because of a natural biological dysfunction.

Although the Greeks knew of superstitions about a woman's menstrual period, they never legislated social laws to separate the sexes during this recurring phenomenon.[15] Jewish purity laws prohibited any type of physical relationship between the sexes during a woman's period. If she so much as touched another person during her period, she would infect the other who would, like her, be segregated from all people. This segregation among the unclean would last at least one night and perhaps for even a week (Lev. 15:19-24).

Jacob Neusner researched the practice of *niddah* or "banishment" of woman during her period among literature that predates the writings in the New Testament.[16] He discovered that menstrual taboos were maintained and at times escalated by highly conservative religious sects within Judaism. For instance, at the Qumran settlement near the northwest edge of the Dead Sea, the Zadokites criticized the priests working at the temple in Jerusalem for sleeping with menstruating women:

> Inasmuch as they do not keep separate according to the law but lie with her that sees the blood of flux.[17]

The first-century Jewish historian, Josephus, as well as writings attributed to Philo of Alexandria, another important Jewish writer, approve and uphold purity laws for women.[18] The *Talmud*, an ancient Jewish book of law and legend, requires strict adherence to these ancient menstrual laws.[19]

This sexual segregation was central to the beliefs and practices of the ancient Jews. Just as circumcision was the sign of a covenant member who could become a priest and thus lead the people, menstruation—a natural biological function—proved to be an exclusionary sign for a woman. Woman however gifted would never gain access to the inner sanctuary of the temple. Nor could she ever officially represent God to her people.

Purity laws could prevent both sexes from establishing a meaningful personal relationship. The sexes functioned in different worlds with different duties. Even at the joyous occasion of the birth of a child the sexes were warned to remain separate. Women were cloistered for at least sixty-six days after the birth of a female and thirty-three days after the birth of a male (Lev. 12:1-13). These exclusionary practices weve even maintained among Sadducean Jews during the first century A.D. (C.E.).

While these laws excluded women from priestly functions and cloistered them every month and at the births of their children, they elevated men to a lonely position of power (Lev. 8-9). Women and men, although married, although permitted to have physical relations for at least one half of each month, were at least potentially isolated from each other.

Men and women were discouraged from talking with each other in public. While some women did obtain an education, it was in complete isolation from men. The *Talmud* preserves many traditions about irate men that neither understood nor appreciated women. From a distance they feared them, yet at other times they worshiped them.[20]

Mark addresses the issue of sexual segregation by telling the story of the Hemorrhaging Woman. She breaks many of the rules. Even though she is "unclean" and "infectious," she reaches out, touches, and finally converses with Jesus in public.[21] Her actions are rewarded with health.

The woman's illness has lasted for 12 years. She has a "scourge."[22] She should not be one of the thronging masses following Jesus. Every person she touches will be "infected." She ignores the ancient taboos and touches Jesus.

Her touch reaches Jesus' garment. Matthew and Luke say that she touched "only" the "hem" of his garment (Matt. 9:18-26; Luke 8:40-56). In the Old Testament the fringe of the garment reminded the Jews that they must keep all of Yahweh's laws (Num. 15:37-39; Deut. 22:12).

Mark's story concentrates on the physical as well as social oppression of this woman. Mark is concerned with her medical history that has left her without funds (Mark 5:26). Luke only briefly alludes to it, and Matthew discards it. Mark suggests that the ineptitude of her physicians has increased her emotional as well as physical discomfort.

Many ancient writers would agree with this view of physicians. Heraclitus in the sixth century B.C.E. writes this about medical healers,

> Physicians who cut and burn, demand payment of a fee, although undeserving, since they produce the same [pains as the disease].[23]

According to the *Mishna*, Jewish tractates contained in the Talmud, "the best of the physicians deserved hell."[24]

She has a "scourge." The term is both picturesque and ironical. Jesus is scourged as well as martyred in the book of Hebrews (Heb. 12:6). The image is of a person who is beaten to the point of no resistance—perhaps even death. Is Mark indirectly comparing the humiliating death of Jesus with the social outrage and physical pain this woman has experienced? (See Mark 3:10; Luke 7:21; Acts 22:24; Heb. 11:36).

By including this story, Mark may be suggesting that there should be no sexual segregation. Jesus does not walk away from her. Neither does he beat her because she has broken the ancient purity restrictions. He graciously recognizes her.

In the Greek the feminine form of the interrogative pronoun is used in the phrase, "Who touched me?" (Mark 5:31). Jesus recognizes the touch of a woman. Her touch does not merit a reprimand but an applause. Jesus addresses her in public and even calls her "daughter" (Mark 5:33-34).

Mark takes this fractured and isolated woman and tells a story that moves her from anonymity to family member, from an impersonal relationship with Jesus to a personal one, from complete disruption in her personal, social, and cultic life to a total state of wholeness. "Your faith has made you well" (5:34).

Mark bridges the chasm between woman and man, and woman and cult. The woman is featured for her faith in spite of her biological dysfunction. She is not only part of the community but she becomes a witness to that community who remembers Jesus. And that community should supply the basis and energy for physical, emotional, and social wholeness. Women and men need never to be separated again.

The Hemorrhaging Woman as Faith Healer

This woman's faith is radical. It has puzzled readers and interpreters of the Bible for centuries. Long ago, Chrysostom believed that her faith was far superior to that of the disciples.[25] Indeed she seems to have knowledge and intuitive abilities that no one else claims in Mark's story. Even Jairus falls short when it comes to faith.

This story about Jairus and his daughter encircles the story about the Hemorrhaging Woman.

While he was by the lakeside, the president of one of the synagogues came up, Jairus by name, and, when he saw him, threw himself down at his feet and pleaded with him. "My little daughter," he said, "is at death's door. I beg you to come and lay your hands on her to cure her and save her life." So Jesus went with him . . . .

While he was still speaking, a message came from the president's house, "Your daughter is dead; why trouble the Rabbi further?" But Jesus, overhearing the message as it was delivered, said to the president of the synagogue, "Do not be afraid; only have faith." After this he allowed no one to accompany him except Peter and James and James's brother John. They came to the president's house, where he found a great commotion, with loud crying and wailing. So he went in and said to them, "Why this crying and commotion? The child is not dead: she is asleep"; and they only laughed at him. But after turning all the others out, he took the child's father and mother and his own companions and went in where the child was lying. Then, taking hold of her hand, he said to her, "*Talitha cum*," which means, "Get up, my child." Immediately the girl got up and walked about—she was twelve years old.   (Mark 5:21-24; 35-42, NEB)

Jairus (the awakened or enlightened one)[26] seems to be illuminated by the Hemorrhaging Woman. Jairus, like the woman, comes to Jesus for help. His daughter is dying. Before Jesus reaches Jairus' home, she succumbs to her illness and dies (Mark 5:23, 35). He is helpless. Unlike the woman, he was unable to tap into the divine energy to save his daughter. How ironic for this synagogue chief—a religious ruler—to fail in matters of faith. The Hemorrhaging Woman succeeds even though her illness would have prevented her from worshiping with him in his synagogue.[27]

Jairus needs encouragement, the woman does not. Jesus says to Jairus, "Do not fear, only believe" (Mark 5:36, RSV). To the woman no encouragement is given. She pursues Jesus. She touches him. She believes and she is healed. "Your faith has made you well" (Mark 5:34, RSV). Jairus believes he must wait for the touch of Jesus. He is like the twelve who are frightened on the lake (Mark 6:45-52) and who do not understand how to heal the young possessed boy (Mark 5:28). He is powerless.

The woman also fears but is not paralyzed (Mark 5:33). Her faith was so strong it appears that she was in control of the healing powers found in Jesus. Her healing seems to be an involuntary act by Jesus (Mark 5:30).[28]

According to this story in Mark, "power" is available not only to Jesus but to those who have a special gift or strength. Neither the twelve nor Jairus seem to use this special gift. Yet Mark includes stories about other people not in the immediate circle of Jesus who are doing wondrous things called "powers." "No one who does a miracle in my name can in the next moment say anything bad against me, for whoever is not against us is for us" (Mark 9:39-40, NIV).[29]

The Hemorrhaging Woman's power is a divine mystery to some,[30] yet to others it is a story about how faith can cure even the most dreaded of diseases. To some it is a story about a woman who had the courage to pursue, touch, believe, and be healed.[31] An ancient church historian, Eusebius of Caesarea, preserved a legend about the house of this courageous and daring woman. Apparently it had become a shrine.

> But since I have come to mention this city (Caesarea Philippi), I do not think it right to omit a story that is worthy to be recorded also for those who come after us. For they say that she had an issue of blood, and who as we learn from the sacred Gospels found at the hands of our Savior relief from her affliction, came from this place, and that her house was pointed out in the city, and that marvelous memorials of the good deed, which the Savior wrought upon her, still remained. For (they said) that there stood on a lofty stone at the gates of her house a brazen figure in relief of a woman, bending on her knee and stretching forth her hands like a suppliant, while opposite to this there was another of the same material, an upright figure of a man, clothed in comely fashion in a double cloak and stretching out his hand to the woman; at his feet on the monument itself a strange species of herb was growing, which climbed up to the border of the double cloak of brass, and acted as an antidote to all kinds of diseases. This statue, they said, bore the likeness of Jesus. And it was in existence even to our day, so that we saw it with our own eyes when we stayed in the city.[32]

Not only was the memory of Jesus preserved at this shrine; no one would forget this woman. In the story of the Hemorrhaging Woman Jesus recognizes the healing only after it has already taken place within the woman (Mark 5:34). Jesus' last response to her, "Go in peace" (Mark 5:34), is an active command, not a passive salutation. Another acceptable translation would be "Go make peace." She is at peace, therefore she can live and demonstrate peace to others.

Mark's gospel salutes this woman with intuitive powers. She becomes an example of one who can heal through faith. Her story must have been a source of inspiration to a community torn by lack of faith in themselves and their God. Through this story Mark teaches the readers that they can and should have faith in themselves. They can overcome in spite of all the odds. They too can become healthy members of the family of God.

The Hemorrhaging Woman is only one story about the people so valued by Mark. The following few pages will discuss other people. People who exhibit courage, and personal endurance for the communities. Mothers, daughters, widows, itinerant travelers, and mothers-in-law become examples. They are commendable followers of the ancient ways of Jesus.

Mothers, Widows, and Traveling Women

Like the ancient Greeks, many feminists today are offended by the term "servant."[33] Their outrage extends to both the local church and the New Testament.[34] They claim that they have been servants all of their lives. First they were servants to their brothers and fathers when they were children. Then as they chose marriage they became servants to their husbands and their children. They have given up their own personal ambitions and satisfactions in order to help others. They will point to the local church and the members who consistently serve others. It is the women who willingly serve the food, take care of the needs of the children, and even mow the grass on Saturdays.

Feminists do not want to hear about a gospel that centers on service. They have played that game too long. They think it is time for them to be part of the decision-making process of life. They no longer want to be servants and sit in the backseat.

Valeria Saiving in her essay published in 1960 agrees with these women.

> A mother who rejoices in her maternal role—and most mothers do most of the time—knows the profound experience of self-transcending love. But she knows, too, that it is not the whole meaning of life.... The moments, hours, and days of self-giving must be balanced by moments, hours, and days of withdrawal into, and enrichment of, her individual selfhood if she is to remain a whole person. She learns, too, that woman can give too much of herself, so that nothing remains of her own uniqueness; she can become merely an emptiness, almost a zero, without value to herself, to her fellowmen, or, perhaps even to God.[35]

Mark teaches service. Service is the heart of the gospel, yet tasks of giving to others are virtually discarded by society today. And those who continue to give, find little regard or reward from their peers. Even for Mark, as in the example of Jesus, service was not rewarded (Mark 16:1-8).

In order to completely understand Mark, the reader would need to venture back in history through a time warp. We will never comprehend completely what it was like to live in the first century nor to watch Jesus die. The writer of Mark and apparently many others in the first century A.D./C.E. viewed martyrdom and self-denial as essential. Belonging to the community gathered in Jesus' name meant taking a "risk." Jesus says in Mark, "If anyone comes after me, that one must take up his or her cross and follow me" (Mark 8:34). Jesus also says, "The Son of Man did not come to be served but to serve, and to give up his life as a ransom for many" (Mark 10:45, NEB). If everyone who followed Jesus had understood these words in a literal way and the social situation had remained the same, then logically, Christianity would never have survived. Martyrdom would have been the center of this early religion. Why then does Mark uphold such a self-sacrificial model for the readers of this gospel?

One answer may be found in Mark's personal experience of war and violence.[36] Thousands of Jews died as Titus surrounded and finally stormed the city of Jerusalem. Christians fled. No one knows all of the stories about these early followers of the way of Jesus. Self-sacrificial lifestyles might have been a necessity if these people were to survive the turmoil and aftermath of the Jewish Wars. Perhaps Mark recalled these teachings of Jesus because the way of violence had failed so miserably.

It is not easy to deal with Mark's words because they do not seem to fit our time, our own situation in life. We are not facing the things that early readers faced. Their own deaths or the deaths of their friends may have been similar to Jesus' story. Perhaps they could identify with a crucified Jesus because they themselves and their families were threatened with the same end.

Jesus is a servant and he does die. He sets the tone, the example, for the community by giving and dying. In Mark's story there are others who follow Jesus. Among those people are the women. Women "serve" more often than any other character except Jesus (1:31; 15:41).[37]

Woman denies herself, takes up her own cross, and follows Jesus without hesitating or grieving for her former life. She is an answer to the failings of the twelve and others. Mark's stories are about women who actively pursue Jesus and attempt to fulfill the strenuous requirements of this first-century community. The first story remembered by Mark is about a mother-in-law.

The Mother of Simon's Wife

The mother of Simon's wife was healed at the touch of Jesus.

> Simon's mother-in-law was ill in bed with fever. They told him about her at once. He came forward, took her by the hand, and helped her to her feet. The fever left her and she waited upon them. (Mark 1:31, NEB)

Immediately after her return to health "she waited on them"? Most commentators view this phrase in what they see as a proper perspective for all women. They usually indicate that she cooked dinner or pressed their togas for the next day's work. They almost never consider why Mark associates the word *serve* here with this rejuvenated woman. In all probability the word *serve* is one of the most important words for Mark.

Some writers, like Howard C. Kee, suggest that this mother-in-law may have taken care of Jesus' needs on a regular basis. It may have been an avocation or occupation.[38] I believe Professor Kee comes very close to what Mark is intimating in this little miracle story.[39]

Mark is suggesting that this woman is a follower of Jesus. By using the term *serve*, she is identified as one of those people who is attempting to live out Jesus' ideals of servanthood. This does not necessarily mean that her job only includes menial labor. A study of the word *to serve* in the Gospel of Mark reveals that it is only used of Jesus, angels, and women. Mark is making a statement to the community about the qualifications and dedication of women.

In our culture today we do not like the word *serve*. Although many economists are predicting that our society must expand in the area of service functions in order for our economy to remain healthy, we do not like the idea of waiting on another person. We do not reward service-oriented careers in our country. Traditionally these people receive the lowest wages. Yet other writers in the New Testament praise people who are servants. Paul is not ashamed to say that he "served." Timothy and Erastus are termed "servants" of Paul. The word *servant* finds its place between *prophet* and *teacher* in the Book of Romans (Rom. 12:7). Service for Matthew is service to humankind. Food, shelter, and help to the ill and those in prison centers is service.[40]

It is notable that Mark claims life-sustaining activity to beings termed angels (Mark 1:13; 2:1-8; 12:25; 13:27, 32). We will never know the identity of these beings. Yet Mark holds them up to the readers as examples of concern for others.

Women not only serve; they also follow. Their following

does not end at the cross. They continue their allegiance to Jesus in spite of all odds. They never give up.

Women Followers

Mark uses the term *serve* only once again in reference to women.

> A number of women were also present, watching from a distance. Among them were Mary of Magdala, Mary the mother of James the younger and of Joseph, and Salome, who had all followed him and waited on him when he was in Galilee, and there were several others who had come up to Jerusalem with him.
> (Mark 15:40-41, NEB)

Mark says that a number of women both served and followed Jesus. Translators suggest that the role of women at the death of Jesus was menial and minimal. But the writer of Mark did not preserve this tradition about women so the audience would know that Jesus was well-fed and clothed. This episode suggests that they, like other disciples, left their homes and families in order to be with and listen to Jesus. Mark retains the names of only three fervent women, but he recalls that there were many others that should also be remembered.

These women came to Jerusalem with Jesus. *The New English Bible* reads "and there were several others." It should read "several other women," because the form that is used in the Greek is feminine. In Mark, that all-female following had persisted with Jesus since his early days in Galilee. Mark does not say that they followed "behind" but that they were "with him," as associates.

The translators of the *The New English Bible* suggest that women were not intimately involved with the death of Jesus. They were in no way threatened by the brutal scene because they gazed securely from a distance. I believe this is a misinterpretation and a mistranslation. The text could read, "A number of women from a distance were present, watching." This translation emphasizes their place of origin rather than their proximity to the cross. It also fits better with the last part of the verse, "who had all followed him . . . when he was in Galilee."[41] These were the vigilant ones who had not abandoned Jesus.[42]

These women not only served and stayed with Jesus until his death; they also followed him. The term *follow* is a technical word for becoming an associate of Jesus. The first five disciples as well (as many others) make this commitment by "following" Jesus. Simon, Andrew, James, John, and Levi received a personal invitation from Jesus (Mark 1:17-18; 2:14). Other followers included a huge crowd, disciples, Bartimaeus, tax collectors, and even sinners. There are no direct personal invitations to women in Mark. Yet they serve and follow Jesus, just like many others.

While many followed Jesus, they did so for a variety of reasons. Not all were happy with their decisions. Peter complained about his losses (Mark 10:28). And a potential associate of Jesus could not give up his affluent lifestyle; giving all to the poor was too much of a price to pay (Mark 10:17-22). This de-emphasis on materialism (and the emphasis on a continual association with the movement) is present throughout Mark's story. In Mark, women never abandon Jesus nor do they refuse to give of their goods or themselves. They set an example of personal giving for all who would listen to Mark's story.

The Widow

Mark hesitates to flatter the affluent for their lavish contributions to others. Rather, Mark tells a story about a disadvantaged woman who freely gives even though she may be risking her life.

> Once he was standing opposite the temple treasury, watching as people dropped their money into the chest. Many rich people were giving large sums. Presently there came a poor widow who dropped in two tiny coins, together worth a farthing. He called his disciples to him. "I tell you this," he said: "this poor widow has given more than any of the others; for those others who have given had more than enough, but she, with less than enough, has given all that she had to live on."   (Mark 12:41-44, NEB)

This widow—one of the poor who should have been supported by the "rich" or the "affluent disciple"— ironically is one who knows how to give (Mark 10:17-22). She, as a poor person, is an example of total generosity. Mark says that she contributed all of her earthly possessions, her life. "Life" in this context means more than just money; it implies that she had nothing left. She gave it all. This term for life is never used again in Mark. Howard C. Kee believes that Mark's de-emphasis on materialism is an antidote to a tendency in the community to prefer rank and honor over the individual worth of a person. He thinks that the story about this widow is a warning about the "hypocritical disparity between the pious ostentation of the scribes and their inward avarice and inhumanity."[43] While Mark may be targeting one special interest group, the message is the same to all who would read it. This woman, a penniless widow, is an example of self-denial and faithful courage to all the community. She, like the woman who anointed Jesus, is a generous woman who gives and gives and gives.[44]

The Remembered Woman

Mark consistently portrays women in constructive serving roles: they serve, they give of themselves, and they follow Jesus. The Remembered Woman is no exception. She is a nameless woman, like the Hemorrhaging Woman who touched Jesus. She offers oil to Jesus. Her efforts are met with hostility by those who witness her activities.

> Jesus was at Bethany, in the house of Simon the leper. As he sat at table, a woman came in carrying a small bottle of very costly perfume, pure oil of nard. She broke it open and poured the oil over his head. Some of those present said to one another angrily, "Why this waste? The perfume might have been sold for thirty pounds and the money given to the poor"; and they turned upon her with fury. But Jesus said, "Let her alone. Why must you make trouble for her? It is a fine thing she has done for me. . . . She has done what lay in her power; she is beforehand with anointing my body for burial. I tell you this: wherever in all the world the Gospel is proclaimed, what she has done will be told as her memorial."
>
> (Mark 14:4-9, NEB; see also Matt. 26:6-13)

This hostility is not new. Peter shows contempt for Jesus when he is told of his impending crucifixion (Mark 8:32-

34) and the disciples begrudgingly try to keep children away from Jesus (Mark 10:13-16). Matthew agrees that guests treated her with something less than the respect she deserved (Matt. 26:9).

According to Mark the woman should be applauded. "She has done a beautiful thing to me" (Mark 14:6, 8, RSV). She willingly gave of her belongings (oil was very expensive). Although the word *serve* is not used specifically in this context, it is a word that characterizes her activities. She serves by preparing Jesus' body for burial. He is the only person that receives the oil. It is a celebration of his death. According to Mark other followers prepared their teacher for burial. For instance, "John's disciples came and took his body and laid it in a tomb" (Mark 6:29, NIV).

She is to be remembered as no other, not even one of the twelve. Her actions will be part of the story of the gospel. While we might quickly pass over this story, Mark contrasts Judas' lust for money with her wholehearted display of affection. Eventually Judas sells his soul and a friend for a few dollars (Mark 14:10-11).

The Remembered Woman was ostracized for her devotion to Jesus. So too are other women like the Mother of the daughter from Syrophoenicia and the Hemorrhaging Woman who are outcasts of society. Mark recognizes their gifts as essential contributions to the community.

A Mother and a Daughter

Mark breaks down both religious and racial barriers when the stories of the Hemorrhaging Woman and the Mother of the daughter from Syrophoenicia are preserved. In comparing these two stories several important similarities surface.[45] First read this compelling story.

Then he left that place and went away into the territory of Tyre. He found a house to stay in, and he
would have liked to remain unrecognized, but this
was impossible. Almost at once a woman whose
young daughter was possessed by an unclean spirit
heard of him, came in, and fell at his feet. (She was a
Gentile, a Phoenician of Syria by nationality.) She
begged him to drive the Spirit out of her daughter.
He said to her, "Let the children be satisfied first; it is
not fair to take the children's bread and throw it to the
dogs." "Sir," she answered, "even the dogs under the
table eat the children's scraps." He said to her. "For
saying that, you may go home content; the unclean
spirit has gone out of your daughter." And when she
returned home, she found the child lying in bed; the
spirit had left her.   (Mark 7:24-30, NEB)

The quests of the Hemorrhaging Woman and the
Mother of the possessed daughter seemed insur-
mountable.[46] Both women are introduced to Jesus through
hearing and both fall before Jesus (Mark 5:33; 7:25). Jesus
converses in public with both women.[47] Both women
exhibit an enterprising quick-wittedness in their ability to
understand their own personal dilemma.[48] Both were
considered ritually unclean by Jewish cultic standards
(Mark 5:30; 7:27-30). The Hemorrhaging Woman should
have been secluded because of her gynecological disease
and the Mother was a foreigner who would not have kept
the purity regulations.

T. A. Burkill claims that the story about this concerned
Mother was preserved because it portrays Jesus breaking
the Jewish purity regulations.

The introduction of the northerly journey at Mark 7:24 is probably motivated by a desire on the evangelist's part to provide an illustration of Jesus' freedom from the regulations regarding ceremonial cleanliness. Being unhampered by the ancient laws of external purity, the Lord can move into a foreign territory, enter a house there and communicate saving grace to a pagan, thereby anticipating the church's mission to the Gentile world.[49]

If Mark was merely concerned with reaching out to non-Jews, then a story about a non-Jewish man would have been sufficient. Mark may have chosen a story about a non-Jewish woman because the social barriers and religious traditions were twice as difficult to overcome.[50] Jesus breaks the barriers of ancient traditions and offers a new kind of lifestyle that should include others that have been ostracized by society. Both of these women were outcasts. Yet they proved to be reliable and capable persons.

Their active pursuit of Jesus resulted in health. Once again Mark claims that strength and success belong to certain women. Emotional as well as physical endurance are also present in the story about a most hearty woman who was married to seven men.

The Woman Who Married Seven Brothers

The women in Mark's stories survive death, disease, and social ostracism. Here is a story about a woman who survived the death of seven husbands.

And Sadducees came to him, who say that there is no resurrection; and they asked him a question, saying,

"Teacher, Moses wrote for us that if a man's brother dies and leaves a wife, but leaves no child, the man must take the wife, and raise up children for his brother. There were seven brothers; the first took a wife, and when he died left no children; and the second took her, and died, leaving no children; and the third likewise; and the seven left no children. Last of all the woman also died. In the resurrection whose wife will she be? For the seven had her as wife." Jesus said to them, "Is not this why you are wrong, that you know neither the scriptures nor the power of God? For when they rise from the dead, they neither marry nor are given in marriage, but are like angels in heaven.[51]   (Mark 12:18-24, RSV)

This is another of Mark's social commentaries. Clouded beneath the obvious theological arguments about the resurrection is a biting critique of the male-dominated society that bought and sold women as property.

Traditional commentaries focus on the obvious theological questions in this story: resurrection, heaven, and sexuality/marriage.[52] The Sadducees come to Jesus with a trick question about the resurrection because, says Mark, they do not believe in the resurrection. In the ancient Hebrew world some believed that only males could enter heaven. After all they were the covenant members and only they were circumcised. Augustine, an early church writer, comments on this belief.

The Lord denied that there would be in the resurrection not women but marriages; and he uttered this denial in circumstances in which the question would have been more easily and speedily solved by denying that the female sex should exist, if this had in truth been foreknown by him.[53]

Other interpreters zero in on the Levirate law. This Hebrew law demanded that the next surviving male brother or heir should take the deceased man's wife as his own. In early days this law was designed to guarantee children for the brother and to protect the woman, who may not have had her own resources or a means of earning a living. Without such a law she may have had to turn to prostitution or sell herself into slavery.[54]

Evelyn and Frank Stagg have suggested that the central issue of this story is deathlessness and sexual relations. If everyone lived forever, there would be no need for reproduction, no need for sexual differentiation.[55] For Howard C. Kee it is a negative view of marriage.[56] Paul Jewett thinks that it has nothing to do with people living together in this world, since the emphasis is on marriage in that other-world, heaven.[57]

Although these theological questions are important, Mark thinks that social injustices are equally as important. The absurdity of this story should trigger the reader to think beyond the obvious. The question, "Whose wife will she be?" (Mark 12:23) is rather startling. Is this an important question? Is this the real question or is it a facade for other questions? Are they challenging Jesus' stance toward the inclusion of women in this ancient community?

Logically, in the resurrection (if there was a bodily resurrection), this woman would end up with seven husbands. How would she choose among the brothers? Would they all live together? This situation would present quite a problem for the male-dominated society of Mark's time. Hebrew social custom limited the woman to one husband at a time, whereas the man had the choice of one or many. Seldom did the woman make the choice of her lover and husband.[58] Usually it was the Hebrew male who made the final decision.

In this story would she make the choice among the brothers? Is this a question of power and autonomous authority? Or is this a question of ownership? If all had her as wife, will they all share her in the resurrection? Who will have property rights? Who will have the benefit of her company or the responsibility of her upkeep?

Jesus' answer is revolutionary for the first century. "When they rise from the dead, men and women do not marry; they are like angels in heaven" (Mark 12:25, NEB). The angels are not differentiated by sex, religion, or social upbringing (see Mark 1:2; 1:13; 8:38; 13:27). Mark blasts the Hebrew social code that potentially confined women to a passive existence in their society and cultic activities. In the Hebrew world women had to bear the burden of a religious social system that was instituted by males and was for the primary benefit of males.

This story breaks open this male-oriented system by presenting a condition where woman might have authority over the men in her life. Instead of claiming female superiority (after all the woman did outlive all seven brothers), the writer prefers equality. The main point of the story is that people should not receive privileges just because of their sex. In the resurrection there will be no need for social laws to take care of women. They will serve with vigor, strength, and dedication as the angels—as the Hebrew men have done for centuries. Life in the resurrection will be active and productive. All will share in an equal partnership in an open-ended community.

Mark's stories about women provide an ancient glimpse of successful people. They overcome. They serve. They follow. They love and care for their families and friends. They have faith that can cure themselves and perhaps others. They are considered to be equally capable and responsible in the developing community. Mark does not call women "leaders," but on almost every page they are presented as important people. The final portrayal of women is a sad but hopeful tale. They watched Jesus die. They stood by his side at the grave and at last they listened to words of hope. Jesus will return.

Daughter as Leader

As the worshipers of Apollo looked to the Oracle at Delphi, so it is to the women that the community should turn in order to find a voice from the Divine. In the Greco-Roman world the emotions and bodily reactions of trembling were usually interpreted as signs of the presence of God.[59]

> Then the woman, knowing what had happened to her, came and fell at his feet and, trembling with fear, told him the whole truth.   (Mark 5:33, NIV)

There is a personal moment between Jesus and the Hemorrhaging Woman. She is individually featured before the crowd (the witnessing community). Her response to this event is fear and trembling (Mark 5:33).

This anxious reaction can be interpreted in a variety of ways. H. B. Swete and A. M. Hunter think that she may be presumed to be confessing her sinful condition and activities,[60] although the word *sin* is never mentioned in the story. Others think that fear and trembling is a natural reaction to a miraculous cure. Some say that this fear demonstrated by the women at the tomb paralyzed them; "they said nothing to anyone, for they were afraid" (Mark 16:8, RSV).[61] Yet Mark uses the word *fear* in an earlier narrative to describe very active followers of Jesus:

> They were on the road; going up to Jerusalem, Jesus leading the way; and the disciples were filled with awe, while those who followed behind were afraid.
> (Mark 10:32)

Fear is a part of the lives of the people who follow Jesus. It does not stop them along their journey. The text reads, "who followed behind." *Behind* here is an unwarranted addition by the translator. It places the followers at a distance or suggests that there were two groups of people who followed Jesus, those that feared (filled with awe) and those that did not fear. Mark makes no such distinction. Fear is a proper response to the Divine, says Mark (4:40-41). Fear does not necessarily paralyze. It can be a response to Jesus' activities or crowd hysteria.[62] H. Betz sees it as a divine intervention into the human world.[63] Mark appears to say that it is an appropriate response to God. It comes as people attempt to follow the ideals of Jesus.[64]

According to ancient Hebrew law, no woman by herself was allowed to be a witness, either in business matters or in court.[65] The Hemorrhaging Woman, in front of a crowd, tells the "truth." The lone Women at the Tomb (Mark 16:5-7) hear a message of truth..

Peter: "He is going on before you into Galilee; there you will see him, as he told you."   (Mark 16:7, NEB)

Ironically, women are chosen to bring the hopeful message to the disciples and Peter. The twelve forfeited their privileged place by abandoning and denying Jesus. Yet they are not forgotten. They will receive a message from the Divine by way of the women.

The women responded with fear, trembling, and silence (Mark 16:8).[66] This is consistent within Mark's narrative. Women rarely speak audibly. Throughout all of the woman-traditions Mark highlights the acts of women. Speaking does not always imply understanding. For instance, Peter correctly calls Jesus "Messiah," yet he did not correctly discern the meaning of that title (Mark 8:9). The Mother from Syrophoenicia correctly perceived the person of Jesus. She calls him "Lord."[67] Her display of humility demonstrates her understanding of Jesus (Mark 7:2-28).

It would seem, therefore, to be part of the evangelist's doctrinal intent to suggest that the Syrophoenician woman, in addressing Jesus as Lord, is a presage of things to come. Even during the earthly ministry, before the Messiah's final rejection of his own people, a representative of the religiously underprivileged world can, in a moment of inspiration, recognize Jesus as the Lord of the Christian cultus who offers himself as the bread of life for the salvation of humanity.[68]

Mark preserves very few positive traditions about the twelve. Their leadership has failed. The voice of God should come from those who recognize the Divine and seek to live out the ways of the Divine, of Jesus. Mark upholds the women who recognize, serve, and follow Jesus. They are among those who are preparing "the way of the Lord" (Mark 1:2-3, RSV).

Summary

In the Gospel of Mark, Jesus commanded the Hemorrhaging Woman to go, and the mysterious stranger asked the Women at the Tomb to go—so they went. "The beginning of the gospel of Jesus Christ . . ." (Mark 1:1, RSV) is not with those of the past. Times have changed. Life is different after the fall of Jerusalem. The community must find its leaders among those that know best how to live and love and have faith in each other. Mark portrays ancient women with this kind of talent. The woman traditions preserve reminiscences of courageous lives. The present situation may necessitate silence in word, but not in action. Women become models of healthful living as Mark reflects on Jesus' past. Jesus welcomed the talents of women as they became daughters who lived, taught, and understood the ideals of Jesus.

2

MATTHEW'S STORY

Daughter as Family Member

Tell the daughter of Zion, "Here is your king,
who comes to you in gentleness . . ."
(Matt. 21:5, NEB)

Introduction

Matthew's story is designed to settle and stabilize readers. While Mark left people at the brink of day waiting for Jesus to return,[1] Matthew is convinced that Jesus not only returned from the dead; he gave instructions to people who wanted to follow him. Matthew writes of Jesus' past, present, and future. There is an unspoken surety as Matthew writes about traditions that speak of the strength and authority of Jesus' life and teachings.

Matthew's readers find security and community even though their own world may be in jeopardy. Their beliefs in Jesus are grounded in the most ancient of Hebrew traditions. Jesus was not just another would-be king of Palestine; he was the long-awaited Messiah. This Messiah had the audacity to challenge the legal system of the past,[2] yet lovingly to point people in a new direction of care and family-communal living. This communal living was open to all who needed and wanted to construct a new world (Matt. 28:19-20).[3]

Matthew's nonsectarian concern for humanity is denied by many who claim a Jewish bias for Matthew. They point to pro-Jewish statements that seem to limit the scope of Matthew's view of community. Among them is this statement.

> I was sent to the lost sheep of the house of Israel, and to them alone.[4]   (Matt. 15:24, NEB)

As this chapter unfolds, we will see Matthew's expanding worldview. While the Jewish heritage of Jesus is appreciated, Matthew will not allow it to dominate the present Christian community. Matthew speaks with an audience who understands the conservative Jewish traditions, but those traditions are not allowed to continue to exclude and victimize outsiders.

Woman and Family Living

Family life and women are important to Matthew. Nearly all of the Marcan stories about family find their way into Matthew's gospel.[5] Mothers and fathers are honored in Matthew. (See, for instance, Matthew 10:37, 38; 11:11; 19:18.)

> For God said, "Honour your father and mother," and, "The man who curses his father or mother must suffer death."   (Matt. 15:4, NEB)

And a daughter is brought back to life (Matt. 9:25). Matthew understands a woman's grief and anxiety about her children during war (Matt. 9:18-26; 24:19). Yet the writer also agrees that anxiety and grief can be produced by a mother, like Herodias (Matt. 14:3-12).

Matthew appreciates Mark's choice of woman traditions. Yet Matthew thinks that women should be more of an integral part of the story. Women characters are included in a genealogy (Matt. 1:4-7), as well as in the story of the feedings of the 4,000 and the 5,000 (Matt. 14:21; 15:38). A mother becomes the central character in the dialogue about the quest for power by the sons of Zebedee (Matt. 20:20).

Although Matthew appreciates women and family, it appears that the traditional family unit is threatened by both external and internal divisiveness. The effects of the wars linger on in the ruined family structures. The following paragraph speaks of this alienation, fear, and dissolution:

> Do not think that I have come to bring peace on earth, I have not come to bring peace, but a sword. For I have come to set a man against his father, and a daughter against her mother, and a daughter-in-law against her mother-in-law; and a man's foes will be those of his own household.   (Matt. 10:34-36, RSV)

Matthew remembers how it "was." The writer hopes and pleads for a new kind of life for the people who have survived. That life can no longer be centered around blood-relations. It must be centered in people who have a common cause and care for each other. Family must be reconsidered and redefined if they are to survive. That family will learn to open its arms to people it may have ignored or spurned in the past.

Several stories leave the reader with a feeling of chaos and fear. Jesus does not enter into a peaceful world. Mary and Joseph must escape the torment of Herod who intends to murder all the male children of Bethlehem. Matthew grieves for the children as Rachel's tears are recalled.

> A voice was heard in Rama, wailing and loud laments; it was Rachel weeping for her children, and refusing all consolation, because they were no more.
>
> (Matt. 2:18, NEB)

Tears fall as Matthew ponders the pregnant women caught in the ravages of war.

> Alas for women with child in those days, and for those who have children at the breast!   (Matt. 24:19)

Violence touched all types of women. Matthew remembers a mother whose power was used to kill. The story about Herodias indicates a very unstable political system. Human lives are forfeited on a whim. Matthew views Herodias as the villain who conceives the death wish for John the Baptist because he criticized her personal life. She uses her own daughter to destroy this man.

> Now Herod had arrested John, put him in chains, and thrown him into prison, on account of Herodias, his brother Philip's wife; for John had told him: "You have no right to her." Herod would have liked to put

him to death, but he was afraid of the people, in whose eyes John was a prophet. But at his birthday celebrations the daughter of Herodias danced before the guests, and Herod was so delighted that he took an oath to give her anything she cared to ask. Prompted by her mother, she said, "Give me here on a dish the head of John the Baptist." The king was distressed when he heard it; but out of regard for his oath and for his guests, he ordered the request to be granted, and had John beheaded in prison. The head was brought in on a dish and given to the girl; and she carried it to her mother. Then John's disciples came and took away the body, and buried it . . .

(Matt. 14:3-12, NEB; Mark 6:14-29; Luke 3:19-20)

Unlike Luke, Matthew chooses to preserve this vicious tradition about a royal Roman family. Their hideous practical joke is just another tradition in a long line of violent traditions that create a climate of anarchy. Who could be safe in this kind of environment? Ideally the family should be a place of comfort. It should provide an atmosphere of wholeness, acceptance, and care for family members as well as their friends and acquaintances. Matthew indicates that this is not happening. Although Matthew shifts the desire for the death of John to Herod, it is Herodias that "pulls the switch." She expresses no regret for her abominable act.[6] Capital punishment is now in the hands of unstable people and Matthew's readers are frightened as they watch their own families disintegrate.

Divorce and Marriage

As families disintegrate, children are abandoned and

people declare themselves divorced. Matthew sends an alarming note to potential readers.[7] Two sayings are included on the issue of divorce (Matthew 5:27-32; 19:3-12). Here is one of them:

> And Pharisees came up to him and tested him by asking, "Is it lawful to divorce one's wife for any cause?" He answered, "Have you not read that he who made them from the beginning made them male and female, and said, 'For this reason a man shall leave his father and mother and be joined to his wife, and the two shall become one flesh'? So they are no longer two but one flesh. What therefore God has joined together, let not man put asunder." They said to him, "Why then did Moses command one to give a certificate of divorce, and to put her away?" He said to them, "For your hardness of heart Moses allowed you to divorce your wives, but from the beginning it was not so. And I say to you: whoever divorces his wife, except for unchastity, and marries another, commits adultery."   (Matt. 19:3-9, RSV)

Matthew's version of Jesus' statement on divorce seems intolerable for readers of the gospel today. We hesitate to take such a seemingly narrow view of divorce. We understand divorce. It has its benefits and consequences. Staying in an unhealthy marriage could mean disaster for both partners as well as the children. It is a fact that the majority of murders occur because of domestic disputes. Victims are usually loved ones.[8]

Readers of Matthew have debated the writer's hardline approach to divorce for centuries. Divorce is allowed only on grounds of "unchastity."[9] What does this term mean? Does it refer to adultery, incest, cultic prostitution, marrying outside your religion, or polygamy? No one knows why the writer chose this approach to divorce. The answer may be found in the historical situation. Times were certainly different for Matthew who lived almost two thousand years ago.

Many successful Jews chose to support more than one woman. Usually a family would consist of one legal wife plus concubines or slaves. This type of arrangement worked during affluent times. It worked for Jews that made a good living working at the temple or selling their goods in one of the busy marketplaces within Jerusalem. But after the devastation of Jerusalem, and with it the economic system, many Jews may have been faced with bankruptcy or financial ruin. Ancient historians tell us that the Jews lost their property and their goods. Then a heavy tax was levied against every Jew in the empire.

How could a Jewish man support several other people when there was little left to keep him alive? The dilemma poses overwhelming choices. In times like these Matthew calls for solidarity and responsibility to the family. Matthew seems to say, "Take care of each other. Don't abandon one another except for unchastity. Hold your wives close to you so that all of you can survive the postwar years." At the very least, Matthew hopes for people to stay together in the time of need.

While Matthew's gospel argues for the strength and stature of the marriage bond, there is also an unpredictability about life. Traditional marriage gives way to celibacy (whatever the exact nature),[10] and virginity seems to be a timely topic.[11] The following allegory speaks of the fragility of the times—the waiting, the inability to know the future or to control it, and the hope that is rewarded to some and not to others:

> When that day comes, the kingdom of Heaven will be like this. There were ten girls, who took their lamps and went out to meet the bridegroom. Five of them were foolish, and five prudent; when the foolish ones took their lamps, they took no oil with them, but the others took flasks of oil with their lamps. As the bridegroom was late in coming they all dozed off to sleep. But at midnight a cry was heard: "Here is the bridegroom! Come out to meet him." With that the girls all got up and trimmed their lamps. The foolish said to the prudent, "Our lamps are going out; give us some of your oil." "No," they said; "there will never be enough for all of us. You had better go to the shop and buy some for yourselves." While they were away the bridegroom arrived; those who were ready went in with him to the wedding; and the door was shut. And then the other five came back, "Sir, sir," they cried, "open the door for us." But he answered, "I declare, I do not know you." Keep awake then; for you never know the day or the hour.
>
> (Matt. 25:1-13, NEB)

This allegory about ten virgins seems absurd.[12] Ten female virgins are waiting for one bridegroom. Five make it and five don't. Are they viable candidates for the marriage or are they part of the wedding party? How many men could have afforded to feed and clothe five women even before the Jewish wars?

This allegory remembers troubled times. People are waiting. Choices need to be made. Some are chosen and some are left behind. The same theme occurs in the parable of two women grinding at the mill.

> Then there will be two men in the field; one will be taken, the other left; two women grinding at the mill; one will be taken, the other left.
>
> (Matt. 24:40-41, NEB)

How and why those choices are made is not very clear in Matthew. Perhaps it is a recollection of the wars when some survived and others did not. Matthew's readers understand the fickleness of war (Matt. 22:23-33). These stories and others speak of a dismal time in history. Matthew attempts to rebuild this world by reiterating the traditions of the past, coupled with an openness to build something new for future generations. Standing in the middle of this endeavor are the traditions about women. No matter what their background, status, present situation, or marital status, women are essential family members in the new community.

The New Family

Matthew affirms the traditional, legal, family unit of man and wife, but also preserves traditions that redefine family living and structure. Matthew includes a genealogy (Matt. 1:1-16), an infancy story (Matt. 1:16—2), and changes the story about the brothers and sisters of Jesus (Matt. 12:46-50). All of these reflect a more inclusive approach to family roles and living. They jar the community to an awareness of other people and their lifestyles. Matthew prevents no one from becoming a member of the new community.

Matthew signals this revolutionary ideal in the opening verses of the gospel as some of Jesus' ancient ancestors are listed.

> A table of the descent of Jesus Christ, son of David, son of Abraham.

> Abraham was the father of Isaac, Isaac of Jacob, Jacob of Judah and his brothers, Judah of Perez and Zarah *(their mother was Tamar)*, Perez of Hezron, Hezron of Ram, Ram of Amminadab, Amminadab of Nahshon, Nahshon of Salma, Salma of Boaz *(his mother was Rahab)*, Boaz of Obed *(his mother was Ruth)*, Obed of Jesse; and Jesse was the father of King David.

> David was the father of Solomon *(his mother had been the wife of Uriah)*, Solomon of Rehoboam, Rehoboam of Abijah, Abijah of Asa, Asa of Jehoshaphat, Jehoshaphat of Joram, Joram of Azariah, Azariah of Jotham, Jotham of Ahaz, Ahaz of Hezekiah, Hezekiah of Manasseh, Manasseh of Amon, Amon of Josiah; and Josiah was the father of Jeconiah and his brothers at the time of the deportation to Babylon.   (Matt. 1:1-11, NEB)

Jesus has a long history, according to Matthew, that dates back to David and Abraham. His ancestry claims Jewish royalty and Jewish intrigue. In the midst of this sectarian affirmation of Jesus, Matthew shocks the readers by deviating from traditional genealogical tables. Familiar women—non-Jewish women—are inserted into the prehistory of Jesus. Jews would be familiar with the stories, but they would probably not consider them to be equally viable ancestors of the Messiah (Matt. 1:1-5).[13]

Tamar, Rahab, Ruth, and Bathsheba are neither ideal nor perfect Jewish women. Their stories are packed with adventure, romance, and sometimes fascinating circumstances. Their stories do not fit into the prescribed pattern described by Jewish law. Yet somehow these women are responsible for bringing the Messiah into the world. Matthew includes their names because they fit into the nontraditional family pattern of Jesus' birth, life, and murder.

Several writers think that the inclusion of these women into a traditional patriarchal genealogy underscores a theological purpose of Matthew. M. D. Johnson says, "At least three of the women were considered morally assailable and all four [were] of Gentile ancestry—or at least not full Israelites."[14] For instance: Ruth, a Moabite, was a single woman who, after the death of her husband, chose to live in a foreign land and then chose her own husband. (See the book of Ruth.)[15] Rahab was a Canaanite who lived in the city walls of Jericho. She helped two spies aligned with the Israelites who were waiting in the desert (Josh. 2:1; 6:17). Bathsheba, probably a Hittite, was David's lover and then wife. She eventually bore Solomon who became the next king of Israel. David won her through planning the death of her husband (2 Sam. 11:2-5; 12:24; 1 Kings 1:1-2:25). Several Tamars are mentioned in the Old Testament. In Genesis, Tamar tricks her father-in-law into sleeping with her. She gives birth to children that were illegally denied to her (Gen. 38:6-30). In 2 Samuel, Tamar is the daughter of David. Amnon, her brother, rapes her. For this deed Absalom murders him (2 Sam. 13:1-32). (See also Ruth 4:12.)

Matthew's inclusion of these women raises scores of questions.[16] But the basis for all of these debates rests in the ideals of community prescribed in the opening sentences of Matthew's story. While Jesus is rooted in the best of all ancient Hebrew traditions, Matthew reminds everyone that Jesus could never have been born without the help of these women. Their presence signals the honest declaration that family in the Matthean community is open to all no matter what their race, religious heritage, or sex. Matthew implies that Hebrew males are important, but so are females; and this begins Matthew's view of an androgynous community.[17]

Family Is Androgynous

Matthew affirms traditional family living, yet is open to alternative lifestyles. The narrative about Jesus' birth and Matthew's edition of one saying illustrate this point. Matthew seems to highlight the father of Jesus—Joseph—in the narrative about Jesus' birth and escape (Matt. 1:18-20). Janice Capel Anderson says, "The opening genealogy is patrilineal and the birth stories center on Joseph."[18] Mary finds herself pregnant and Joseph reacts. An angel of the Lord appears and convinces him not to take action against Mary. Subsequently the angel gives Joseph information that eventually leads Jesus and Mary to safety and a safe return after the threat against Jesus' life (Matt. 1:20, 25; 2:13, 19). However, the conclusion that Joseph is the center of the narrative may be hasty. Upon further investigation of Matthew's language, another picture emerges.

Although Joseph assumes a father role in the escape story about Jesus, Matthew highlights Mary in both the genealogy and the flight from Herod. The genealogy says that Joseph was the "husband of Mary" (Matt. 1:16). The line ends with Mary. Joseph's lineage is found in the person of Mary. This genealogical statement is highly unusual for a patriarchal Jewish religion that permitted only the man to acquire a spouse. In the narrative Matthew presents Joseph as being Mary's husband before Joseph accepted her as his wife (Matt. 1:24, 25). According to H. Waetjen, "The displacement of Joseph may relocate the emphasis in the maternity of Mary, but the paternity is not repudiated or contradicted."[19] Both sexes are equally celebrated as participants in the prehistory of Jesus.

Although Joseph is mentioned six times in the birth narrative, the mother of Jesus—Mary—is mentioned seven times (Matt. 1:18, 20; 2:11, 13, 14, 20, 21). She is an essential character. Like Joseph, she also received a message from the angel. Together they leave Bethlehem (Matt. 1:12).

Matthew wants the readers to understand that Jesus had both a father and a mother. Matthew's gospel emphasizes this androgynous background of Jesus. In Mark's story, people begin to wonder about the miraculous powers of Jesus. They begin to discuss his background. As they talk one person says, "Is not this the carpenter, the son of Mary and brother of . . . ?" (Mark 6:3).[20] But Matthew's version includes a father.

> "Is he not the carpenter's son? Is not his mother called Mary, his brothers James, Joseph, Simon, and Judas?

And are not all his sisters here with us?''[21]

(Matt. 13:55, NEB)

Mark narrates a story about only one parent. Matthew traces Jesus' lineage to both a woman and a man.

While Matthew may appear to the reader to be patriarchal, it does not seem intentional. Matthew is speaking to a community with Jewish roots. Matthew must use language that will communicate with readers of the gospel. The writer does what we do not expect. Ancient doors are opened by breaking open the male-dominated religious heritage of the Jews. Although Matthew's language is steeped in tradition, it offers a forward-looking stance toward women and others that was neglected by the ancient religious heritage.

Matthew has set the tone for the gospel by telling a story about a person who has an ancient historical heritage that includes a diversity of people. Jesus' present and future will be like his past. He will welcome all into the new community. This community is both androgynous and inclusive. Women and men are equally important. There is hope for this community that must rely upon all of its members in order to survive.

Woman and the Rebuilding of Community Living

Matthew understands the Jewish exclusive and restrictive heritage of the past. Women were not covenant members of the community. They could not be circumcised. Their biology prevented them from participating in most cultic festivities.[22] These traditions inform the developing Matthean community. But they do not restrain it or hinder it. As Matthew tells the story of Jesus, women are not neglected. Rather they are strategically included within Marcan stories which only featured men.

The following traditions pronounce women as capable, resourceful, and necessary for the community living after the fall of Jerusalem. Matthew recognizes that women have always been present, even though their contributions have not always been celebrated. As the stories are retold by Matthew, Jesus seems to create an even more intimate climate with women.

Matthew's gospel includes women characters in two repetitive Marcan stories: the feeding of the four thousand and the five thousand (Matt. 14:13-21; 15:32:39). Children and women also receive food from Jesus (Matt. 14:21; 15:39). Traditionally Jewish men and women did not eat together in public.[23] Matthew knows that the audience will view this as unusual. They will understand that like the women who are communal receivers of food, so also could they follow Jesus like the chosen disciples. Sharing a meal and listening to Jesus were things that followers did. Women share with the chosen ones and with Jesus—not once but twice.

In the story about the quest for power by the sons of Zebedee, Matthew includes the mother (Matt. 20:20-28). She not only initiates the crucial question of power to Jesus; she remains in the story until his death. She becomes a witness of Jesus' death (Matt. 20:20-28). In spite of her misunderstanding, she, unlike her sons,[24] remains a follower of Jesus until the end. This is the story:

> The mother of Zebedee's sons then came before him, with her sons. She bowed low and begged a favour. "What is it you wish?" asked Jesus. "I want you," she

said, "to give orders that in your kingdom my two
sons here may sit next to you, one at your right, and
the other at your left." Jesus turned to the brothers
and said, "You do not understand what you are asking. Can you drink the cup that I am to drink?" "We
can," they replied. Then he said to them, "You shall
indeed share my cup; but to sit at my right or left is
not for me to grant; it is for those to whom it has already been assigned."   (Matt. 20:20-24, NEB)

Matthew's gospel shifts the blame for the misguided aspirations away from the two "disciples."[25] Their mother
wants Jesus to promote them to positions of influence
within his rule. Mark says that the sons of Zebedee want
Jesus "to do for us whatever we ask of you" (Mark 10:35).
Here in Matthew the mother asks the crucial question, but
it is still on behalf of her sons. She wants power for her
sons, not herself (Matt. 20:21).

Matthew says Jesus responded to her and her sons, "You
do not know what you are asking. Are you able to drink the
cup that I am to drink?" (Matt. 20:22). Mark seems to suggest that these men will face a martyr's death. Matthew
also adds a mother to that group as all respond, "We are
able" (Matt. 20:23). In Mark, the twelve never come to
understand Jesus nor the meaning of his kingdom talk.
Matthew suggests that there may have been women
amidst that puzzled group of followers.

The mother of the sons of Zebedee is not a major
character. She has little else to do with the story until his
death. She witnesses Jesus' crucifixion (Matt. 20:23) but
does not make it to the tomb. What happened to her?
Perhaps she, like the twelve, abandoned Jesus. Or perhaps

she also was martyred for her faith and never lived to see the resurrection.

Matthew's open-ended philosophy toward the acceptance of all people is not novel; the writer of Mark had proposed it twenty years earlier. What is new is Matthew's concentrated effort to convince the readers that women must be part of this all-inclusive community. As women come into the stories, they become increasingly more and more a part of the family of Jesus. Matthew hints that this relationship has a cosmic origin.

For Matthew, family comes from the Father. In the controversial scene where Jesus' mother and brothers come to speak with him, Jesus bursts out, "Who is my mother, and who are my brothers?" (Matt. 12:48). In Mark, this saying seems to be directed toward a very diverse audience. In Matthew, Jesus points his finger directly at the disciples when he speaks. "Here are my mother and my brothers" (Matt. 12:49). Matthew has included women in Jesus' family. They were indirectly included among the disciples. The disciples are a family that came about because of the "will of my Father" (Matt. 12:50; Mark 3:35 says "will of God").

Matthew quietly and cautiously presents women not only in intimate family relationships but also with Jesus. Jesus is portrayed as a strong and divine person. While appreciating the ancient Hebrew past, he is not afraid to break Jewish social laws. Neither is Jesus afraid to be alone with unfamiliar women.[26] Many of the women Jesus meets need help. He is alone with Peter's mother-in-law (Matt. 8:14-15), the ruler's daughter (Matt. 9:25), and the Canaanite woman (Matt. 15:27-28). No other outsiders are integrated into the dialogue that Jesus has with the Hemorrhaging Woman (Matt. 9:20-22). Jesus chooses to "touch" (Matt. 8:15), "grasp"[27] (Matt. 9:25), "converse with" (Matt. 9:22), and "heal" women (Matt. 8:16; 9:21, 25-26). Matthew preserves only one story in which Jesus initially denies help to a woman. It is Mark's story about the Syrophoenician Mother.

> Jesus then left that place and withdrew to the region of Tyre and Sidon. And a Canaanite woman from those parts came crying out, "Sir! have pity on me, Son of David; my daughter is tormented by a devil." But he said not a word in reply. His disciples came and urged him: "Send her away; see how she comes shouting after us." Jesus replied, "I was sent to the lost sheep of the house of Israel, and to them alone." But the woman came and fell at his feet and cried, "Help me, sir." To this Jesus replied, "It is not right to take the children's bread and throw it to the dogs." "True, sir," she answered; "and yet the dogs eat the scraps that fall from their masters' table." Hearing this Jesus replied, "Woman, what faith you have! Be it as you wish!" And from that moment her daughter was restored to health.   (Matt. 15:21-28, NEB)

Matthew understands the social and political tensions among readers of the gospel. Matthew's version more clearly teaches and provokes reflection about religion, race, and sex. According to R. A. Harrisville, the description of the "Canaanite" woman is political in Mark and religious in Matthew.[28] Mark places Jesus at the border of a foreign land and Matthew says that Jesus went into the "parts or districts" of Canaan. According to Hebrew legend, the

Jews were not to associate with Canaanites. Later in Jewish history, when the purity laws were escalated, Jews were forbidden to even touch non-Jews for fear of contamination (Lev. 12—15). By using the word *Canaan*, Matthew stirs up this ancient fear and perhaps hatred of the foreigner, the unknown one—the one that became the enemy of Abraham.[29]

Jesus rejects the woman. While there is a hint of this rejection in Mark, Matthew escalates it. The woman becomes a nuisance as she harasses the disciples. Jesus bitingly retorts, "It is not fair to take the children's bread and throw it to the dogs" (Matt. 15:26).[30] Confronted with all of the Jewish heritage, Jesus at this point opts for a traditional response. "You are not one of us, therefore you cannot benefit from my powers." Jesus does not hold out his hand to this woman in distress, although he does speak with her in public.

The woman will not give up. She humbly begs a "crumb" in order to save her daughter's life. She argues with Jesus and calls him "Son of David."[31] Her argument with Jesus and recognition of this title suggest that she is a very resourceful and intuitive person. No one has recognized Jesus as "Son of David" in the narrative up to this point in Matthew's story. Only two blind men (ironically) see Jesus as being in the line of David. To this list should be added the Pharisees and some within the crowds (Matt. 9:27; 20:30-31; 22:43; 21:9, 15; see also 1:20). The gospel begins with the phrase "The book of . . . Jesus Christ, the son of David" (Matt. 1:1).

Jesus gives in to her demands. He recognizes her strength and says, "Great is your faith" (Matt. 15:28; my translation). A similar phrase is voiced to the non-Jewish centurion, "Truly, I say to you, not even in Israel have I found such faith" (Matt. 8:10). Her daughter is healed.[32]

Matthew uses this provocative story to illustrate a point about the new family gathered after the war in the name of Jesus. Jesus himself learned a lesson from a foreigner. Foreign women, however feared and discriminated against in the past, are a solid contribution to the life of the family. Like the woman from Canaan, they will fight for what is dear to them. They will take care of their children. And they intuitively understand God in ways that the many others could never understand.

As this woman wins health for her daughter, so do all who have such faith. Matthew is proud of the inclusion of different peoples from different worlds into the new Christian community. Jesus' practical healing techniques were inclusive. Barriers tumble as Matthew reaches out to a variety of women. By portraying Jesus as a woman-healer, Matthew is saying that Jesus is a lover of women. Matthew concludes that women—no matter what their past—can and should be significant members of the new family. With an outstretched hand, Jesus reprimands sectarian thinking saying,

> I tell you this: tax-gatherers and prostitutes are entering the kingdom of God ahead of you.
>
> (Matt. 21:31, NEB)

Woman as Courageous Teacher and Family Member

Three stories serve as examples of teaching for Matthew: the Woman who anointed Jesus (Matt. 26:6-13; Mark 14:3-9), the women who follow Jesus to Jerusalem and then watch him die (Matt. 27:55-56), and the women who teach the eleven about the resurrection (Matt. 28:1-10). These traditions provide a fantastic glimpse into Matthew's appreciation for women within the early Christian community. The women are extremely dedicated to Jesus. They risk the embarrassment of being misunderstood. They risk their lives as they watch Jesus die. They stand at the juncture of time and resolutely affirm a future for themselves and their acquaintances. They are remembered as no others are remembered by Matthew. The first story about the woman who anoints Jesus leaves her acts indelibly written on the pages of each canonical gospel.

> Jesus was at Bethany in the house of Simon the leper, when a woman came to him with a small bottle of fragrant oil, very costly; and as he sat at table she began to pour it over his head. The disciples were indignant when they saw it. "Why this waste?" they said; "it could have been sold for a good sum and the money given to the poor." Jesus was aware of this, and said to them, "Why must you make trouble for the woman? It is a fine thing she has done for me. You have the poor among you always; but you will not always have me. When she poured this oil on my body it was her way of preparing me for burial. I tell you this: wherever in all the world this gospel is proclaimed, what she has done will be told as her memorial.'[33]   (Matt. 26:6-13, NEB)

This woman is a teacher. Her activities are questioned but Jesus supports her wholeheartedly. She is not one of the poor. She is one of the affluent who "has done a beautiful thing to me" (Matt. 26:10, RSV). Mark says, "She has done what she could" (Mark 14:8, RSV). She anoints Jesus.

Anointing someone was usually viewed as a powerful action throughout the history of the Jews. Old Testament kings were anointed by a variety of important people (1 Sam. 9:16; 15:1; 2 Sam. 12:7). But Matthew chooses not to use typical words for anointing. Agreeing with Mark, Matthew uses a verb ("to pour") that is associated with kindness, not power or dominion.[34]

The woman anoints Jesus. At that moment hostility erupts toward her. She has wasted the money. There is a confrontation between the disciples and this woman. Jesus chooses to defend the woman against the accusations of his closest followers. He says, "Why must you make trouble for the woman?" (Matt. 26:10, NEB).[35] She understands what is going to happen to him. Like the Canaanite woman who recognizes that he is from the line of David, this woman recognizes that he is going to die. Her warmhearted gift of the oil anointed him in a different way. His kingdom was not grounded on military expansion, or power over people. It was a kingdom that would lead him to the utmost in service—the gift of his life. The woman who anoints, teaches the community to appreciate each other while they have each other. She appreciated Jesus like no other.

The Women at the Cross and the Tomb

Matthew tells two stories about women who, like the saying about the Queen of the South, rise to the occasion (Matt. 12:42). Their lives and activities seem to judge others who are not as daring and dedicated as they are. They follow and serve Jesus and do not abandon him.

> A number of women were also present, watching from a distance; they had followed Jesus from Galilee and waited on him. Among them were Mary of Magdala, Mary the mother of James and Joseph, and the mother of the sons of Zebedee.　　(Matt. 27:55-56)

Matthew agrees with Mark that women watched as Jesus died. Like the Canaanite woman who did not give up hope for her daughter, the women could not abandon Jesus. They had been with him since the days in Galilee (Matt. 27:55-56; Mark 15:40-41).[36]

Why did they stay with Jesus? Were they disciples of Jesus? Both Mark and Matthew say that they followed Jesus (Matt. 27:55; Mark 15:41).

J. D. Kingsbury thinks that their mission was clearly different from the twelve. He bases his conclusion on a study of the term *follow* within Matthew. He says that "to follow" is not a technical term for a disciple of Jesus because it is used once of Jesus following a ruler.[37] Yet, in every other instance in Matthew, "to follow" is used of individuals who are invited to follow Jesus (Matt. 4:20; 25; 9:9; 19:21), the crowds and others who follow (Matt. 4:25; 8:1; 9:27; 12:15; 14:13; 19:2; 20:29; 21:9), or concerning the problems of discipleship and following Jesus (Matt. 8:19-23; 10:38; 16:24; 19:21-28).

G. Kittel disagrees with Kingsbury and says, "The statistical evidence shows that this particular use of *to follow* is strictly limited to discipleship of Christ."[38] Following implies a "self-commitment in a sense which breaks all other ties"[39] and a "participation in the fate of Jesus."[40] Matthew and Mark claim both of these ideals for the women who follow Jesus. They are the closest members of Jesus' family in the Synoptics that witness his death.

Matthew agrees with Mark on the concept of service. "To serve" is a technical term in Mark for those who correctly follow the teachings of Jesus.[41] Both gospel writers emphasize that serving and following must be continuous, and both choose to use different verb tenses in order to communicate this ideal.[42] Matthew agrees with the Marcan thesis that only women, Jesus, and the angels "serve" in the story about Jesus' life (Matt. 4:11; 8:15; 27:55). Matthew outlines in practical terms what it means to serve:

> And they too will reply, "Lord, when was it that we saw you hungry or thirsty or a stranger or naked or ill or in prison, and did nothing for you?" And he will answer, "I tell you this: anything you did not do for one of these, however humble, you did not do for me." And they will go away to eternal punishment, but the righteous will enter eternal life.
>
> (Matt. 25:44-46, NEB)

Caring for others was not generally rewarded in Greek society.[43] Matthew implies that Jesus instituted a "new pattern of human relationships"[44] involving practical, applied love. For the readers of Matthew it became a sign of a true disciple.[45] Matthew claimed that women did all of the above. They were co-workers with Jesus throughout his northern and southern campaigns across Palestine.

These journeys led them to Jerusalem. Mark's story ended on an ironic note. There was only an empty tomb and fearfully silent women who were waiting for Jesus to return. Matthew took Mark's irony and made sense out of it for potential readers.

The sabbath was over, and it was about daybreak on Sunday, when Mary of Magdala and the other Mary came to look at the grave. Suddenly there was a violent earthquake; an angel of the Lord descended from heaven; he came to the stone and rolled it away, and sat himself down on it. His face shone like lightning; his garments were white as snow. At the sight of him the guards shook with fear and lay like the dead.

The angel then addressed the women: "You," he said, "have nothing to fear. I know you are looking for Jesus who was crucified. He is not here; he has been raised again, as he said he would be. Come and see the place where he was laid, and then go quickly and tell his disciples: 'He has been raised from the dead and is going on before you into Galilee; there you will see him.' That is what I had to tell you."

They hurried away from the tomb in awe and great joy, and ran to tell the disciples. Suddenly Jesus was there in their path. He gave them his greeting, and they came up and clasped his feet, falling prostrate before him. Then Jesus said to them, "Do not be afraid. Go and take word to my brothers that they are to leave for Galilee. They will see me there."

(Matt. 28:1-10, NEB)

These women had made contact with the Divine. They fearlessly announce to the world what they have seen at Jesus' grave. Matthew contrasts the women with the guards. "The guards trembled and became like dead men" (Matt. 28:4). The women were not paralyzed. Fear paralyzes Joseph (Matt. 1:20; 2:22), the twelve, at least potentially (Matt. 10:26, 28, 31), Herod (Matt. 14:5), Peter (Matt. 14:27-30), the chief priests and Pharisees (Matt. 21:46), the man in the parable about the talent (Matt. 25:25), but neither the women nor the centurion (Matt. 27:54).

In Matthew, God communicates with women. Mary hears the angel of the Lord (Matt. 1:12) and Pilate's wife has a "dream or vision,"[46] perhaps indicating that she has had an oracle from God. Only women are entrusted with the divine message about Jesus (Matt. 28:5-8). Next Jesus appears to them and encourages them, "Tell my brethren to go to Galilee" (Matt. 28:9-10, RSV). Matthew presents a vivid portrayal of the women rushing off to teach the disciples (Matt. 28:8, 11). The women feared, as in Mark, but they continued to bring the message to others.[47]

This success is heightened when Matthew contrasts the women with the eleven at the end of the story. The women immediately respond to Jesus with worship (Matt. 28:17).[48] They touch Jesus, but the eleven only see him (Matt. 28:10). The eleven are told to make disciples; the women have already begun the process. The women did not doubt, yet some of the eleven "doubted" (Matt. 28:17).

These women are the teachers. They are those within the family of Jesus—the family of Matthew's readers—that can keep a family together. They will pass on the traditions of the past with a loving care that will nourish all the members.

Summary

Matthew includes and celebrates all types of women within the family and community. Women are not an alternative to soured leadership. They are and have been an integral part of the history of Israel and Jesus. They are not something new. The community should know that the presence of women has always been felt within Judaism and now within the early Jesus movement. Courageous women of the past and present serve as ample examples of Christian living and thinking. Unfamiliar women of foreign extraction will serve as models of strength for the future of the church. Their reluctance to give up in the face of disaster is what the community needs. Their peaceful ways will bring healing to everyone.

Matthew does not applaud the strength of women at the expense of men. Both are an essential part of the community. Family life is important. Marriage should be supported with few exceptions. Yet family life is changing and Matthew calls for an openness to new types of communal living and lifestyles. The times require openness.

Although the community has experienced violence, there is hope. There is solidarity in the Jesus traditions that can help to overcome the lingering effects of the wars. Hope and survival depend upon family. Woman is an integral and healthy part of that ideal. She has survived. She does not sway with the wind. She stands true to her beliefs. She can and does carry out the teachings of Jesus. Her life and voice ring out to the readers of Matthew's gospel. Together with the eleven (as a family), they will learn how to "make disciples of *all peoples*" (Matt. 28:19-20). No one needs to shout to the women in Matthew's story,

> Rejoice, rejoice, daughter of Zion, shout aloud, daughter of Jerusalem; for see, your king is coming to you . . .   (Zech. 9:9, NEB)

LUKE'S STORY

Daughter as Friend, Lover, and Companion

*"You gave me no kiss; but she has been kissing
my feet ever since I came in. You did not
anoint my head with oil; but she has
anointed my feet with myrrh.
And so, I tell you,
her great love..."*
(Luke 7:45-47, NEB)

Introduction

Mark's gospel offers a hope for the future. Matthew steadies the readers by linking them to the past and assuring them of a confident present. Luke writes about social injustice and claims a new climate of freedom for both sexes.

Like Matthew and Mark, Luke's gospel betrays violent times.[1] The writer uses both Mark and a collection of sayings of Jesus called "Q."[2] Both of these sources contain an abundance of violent statements and abusive traditions.

Yet Luke does not seem to be writing to or for a people as close to the effects of the wars as Matthew and Mark. The writer attempts to be more objective as the past is reconsidered (Luke 1:1-4). For Luke the present socioeconomic conditions are the most pressing issues.[3]

There is poverty. There is disease. There are people who need help and are not finding it. The rich are not sharing with their neighbors. The religious leaders have ceased to be examples to the people. They are corrupt. They are the generation that should be forgotten.

Times are changing, for Luke's society is rebuilding itself[4] and with that rebuilding comes injustice and oppression. For Luke, women cause neither injustice nor oppression. No parables feature women as the rich who must be criticized. They are never accosted because of their lack of care for the cast-offs of society. They are integral to Luke's message for the readers of this gospel. Their stories find recognition and authority. Women are necessary for the community and its healthy existence.

Women are not on the fringes of the community according to Luke. Neither are they found peaking through the cracks in the temple walls or listening behind doors. Their stories are the foundation myths of Christianity. Their courageous lives are revealed in stories that accentuate their emotions, strength of character, status, and aspirations. Out of a Jewish-Gentile heritage, women stand tall before Luke's congregation.[5]

Luke assumes that women are independent and resourceful. The writer presents the awe-inspiring stories of Mary and Elizabeth. They were mothers but their child-rearing responsibilities did not prohibit them from adding distinctive thoughts and gifts to their communities. The writer tells more stories about widows than any other gospel writer.

Luke admires single women. Mary and Martha support themselves and seem to have the right, obligation, and responsibility to choose their vocations in life. Other women who are in charge of their own private resources support Jesus during his itinerate journeyings (Luke 8:2-3). Many demonstrate love as do no other characters in the Lucan story.

While Mark sees women as an alternative to soured leadership, and Matthew encourages the community to see the historic significance and strength of women within the community, Luke opens the door to new types of relationships and roles within society. The women traditions are powerful stories of successful Christians. Their successes should be appreciated, but as in Matthew, they are not to be worshiped. Women are foundational but so is partnership. Luke attempts to bring the world of woman and man together. The writer hopes that they will listen to each other and work together, for each can contribute to the community.

The key to understanding Luke's view of woman is not found by studying the writer's editing peculiarities. Luke, like Matthew, employs over 60 percent of Mark's gospel.[6] But Luke's genius is best discovered in the material that is distinctively Lucan.[7] While Luke's editorial nuances are important, the following discussion will center on the traditions about woman unique to Luke's gospel.

Mary—the Lucan Mary

The story of the birth of Jesus provides an excellent opportunity for Luke to use personal material to highlight

major characters. The writer features Elizabeth and Mary,
Elizabeth and Zechariah, Zechariah and Mary, Joseph and
Mary, as well as Anna and Simeon. Many writers have
found traces of Hebrew poetry behind the songs and the
narratives.[8] Together these characters become storytellers
as Luke unfolds the life of Jesus. Their heritages are wound
together as the births of two charismatic leaders—John and
Jesus—are told. While all of the characters are important,
Mary is accentuated by Luke. She is the one who coura-
geously chooses, gives, and steps forward out of the background of Jesus' life to become the most important figure
in his childhood.

Who is she? She is a virgin/young woman. She is living
in Nazareth of Galilee. She is betrothed. She has no occupation or trade. According to Luke she has no known background, although she does own her own home. Yet this
woman steps out of the pages of the past to speak and she
does so more than any other character in the infancy narratives.[9]

Throughout the birth accounts, Mary is featured for her
strength of character. She chooses the way of God. Luke
uses many synonyms and adjectives to describe this
unusual woman. She is called "favored" (Luke 1:28). According to J. A. Grassi she receives a new name and a new
life.[10] Luke says, "The Lord is with you" (Luke 1:28). No
other secondary character receives such special praise. She
is called servant, yet she is also blessed (Luke 1:42; 1:38).[11]
Elizabeth Schüssler Fiorenza says that Mary becomes the
hope of the poor.[12] Mary views herself as a very humble
person (Luke 1:48) who is not caught up with her own im-
portance. She often ponders or thinks (Luke 2:19) in her
role as mother (Luke 1:43) and leader of the family.

Hans Conzelmann says plainly, "Mary disappears to a greater extent in Luke than in Mark and Matthew."[13] The following discussion will consider Mary from the Lucan perspective as she is compared with a variety of characters. If she disappears, it is because the interpreter has ignored Luke's vivid and challenging picture of this woman.

Mary and Zechariah

Luke's gospel celebrates life by telling the birth stories of John and Jesus. Most commentators center their questions upon the prophecies told about these two men (Luke 1—4).[14] Subtly Luke tells the story of a hero and a heroine. Luke's community begins to experience the unusual working of God through two characters, Zechariah and Mary. Zechariah and Mary encounter the divine and in their own way they create an atmosphere of wholeness and anticipation about a God that will continue to be active in history.

Luke consciously structures the natives about Zechariah and Mary so that the audience would naturally make a comparison.[15] Mary fascinates Luke, and she gradually begins to dominate the story. Below is a comparison, made by Raymond E. Brown, of the two main characters in the birth narrative.[16]

Zechariah	Mary
Old, childless, and of a priestly family (1:5-7)	A virgin, betrothed, and from the house of David (1:26-38)
Angel of the Lord speaks with him (1:8-23)	Gabriel speaks with her (1:26-38)

A comparison of Luke 1:11-20

Zechariah startled by an angel	Mary startled by Gabriel
Message: Don't be afraid	Message: Favored one, do not be afraid
Elizabeth will bear a son	You will conceive and bear a son
His name will be John	His name will be Jesus
Zechariah receives a sign: He cannot speak	The sign: Your kinswoman has conceived

While there are many similarities between the characters and stories of Zechariah and Mary, Luke portrays Mary (in spite of her humble origins) as significantly more important to the story. Both Elizabeth and Zechariah have the Holy Spirit (Luke 1:15, 41, 67), but the divine overshadows Mary (Luke 1:35). Many scholars see this overshadowing as an allusion to the ark of the covenant in the Old Testament. God indwelled the ark. It was the sign of God working in the world.[17] God is within her.

Zechariah and Elizabeth faced their future together. Luke portrays Mary as alone through the entire annunciation story. Joseph enters only at the birth. Zechariah blesses God, but Mary is called "blessed" (Luke 1:42). Mary is an independent woman who chooses for herself (Luke 1:39). No parents or family are mentioned. After her visit with Elizabeth she returns to her own home (Luke 1:40, 56).

Luke's portrait of Mary is one of appreciation and care for her individuality and strength. She is an independent woman who serves God in a most traditional and natural way. She bears a child. Luke values this contribution as only a part of the total contribution of this woman to the foundation of Christianity.

In spite of her unusual story—a seemingly illegitimate pregnancy—Luke praises this woman. The writer portrays no shame or outrage at her pregnancy. Mary chose to be different, and so she becomes a model for those who would also choose to be different. Her character is admirable. She ponders her choice (Luke 2:19) but never denies it. The audience may be able to identify with this single but promised woman. Individuals are important to God and to the community. Their contribution can exceed even the most dedicated families or couples.

Mary and Elizabeth

Elizabeth is an unusual mother. She is older and child-less. Her hopes and dreams come true at the conception and birth of John. Both Mary and Elizabeth become voices that speak words from God to the readers. Elizabeth is mar-ried and in a patriarchal household (Luke 1:40), yet she names her own child (Luke 1:60-61) in spite of traditions against doing so. In a "loud voice," perhaps indicating divine inspiration, she announces to Mary, "Blessed are you among women, and blessed is the fruit of your womb" (Luke 1:42, RSV).[18]

Elizabeth is a kinswoman of Mary's in many ways (Luke 1:36). She instantly recognizes Mary to be "the mother of my Lord" (Luke 1:43) and understands her happiness as both expect their first child (Luke 1:57; 2:6). Yet Mary's

character and place in the annunciation story again seems
to overshadow Elizabeth's. Here are a few differences and
similarities:

Elizabeth	Mary
Elizabeth is married (1:40)	Mary is betrothed and Joseph enters "with" her (2:5)
Elizabeth understands Mary's significance	Mary understands the future historical and political impact of her child (1:51-55)[19]
A daughter of Aaron (1:5)	From the house of David (1:27; 2:4)
Elizabeth fades into the background after the birth of her child	Mary continues to be an important character through the early years of Jesus' life (2—4)
John is known only as the son of Zechariah (3:2)	Jesus is known in Nazareth as Joseph's son (4:22)

Elizabeth and Mary are two important women for Luke.
Their stories tell the story of Jesus. Their happiness is the
happiness of all who know the story of the Messiah.
Together they step out of traditional roles to add a distinctive tradition to the ancestry of the church. Their active
faith began the Christian traditions, according to Luke.

Mary and Joseph

In Matthew's version of the gospel, the story of Jesus' birth centers in the experience and decision-making of the father, Joseph (Matt. 1—3). The audience meets Mary and knows of her relationship to Joseph, but never has an opportunity to hear her side of the story. Luke's story offers the audience a glimpse of how it all happened from Mary's point of view.

From the beginning of the narrative until the story about Jesus' temptation, Mary is the main character. Her decisions are hers alone. She chooses to conceive and to bear the child (Luke 1:38; 2:7). Joseph's opinion is never registered, although he does bring Mary to Bethlehem in order to register to pay their tax (Luke 2:4).

Luke follows Mary's activities and thoughts. Her name is mentioned first when the shepherds come to visit (Luke 2:16). Often the story breaks away to reveal a concerned and reflective woman. "But Mary treasured up all these things and pondered over them" (Luke 2:19, NEB).

Joseph is Jesus' father and is from the house of David (Luke 2:3; 4:23; 6:42). Luke inserts Joseph into the narrative only as a way to reveal Mary. They are a couple. They are together at the birth of Jesus, his circumcision, and at his presentation at the temple (Luke 2:21). They travel together to Jerusalem, but Mary is always the one who is featured.

Oddly Luke adds a phrase that has puzzled people for centuries:

> When the time of their purification according to the Law of Moses had been completed, Joseph and Mary took him to Jerusalem. (Luke 2:22, NIV)

Normally a Jewish woman was quarantined 33 days at the birth of a male—66 if she bore a female child—in addition to the initial seven and fourteen days. After her time of seclusion, she would then travel to the temple and offer a sacrifice for her sin (Lev. 12:1-8). Luke seems to suggest by using the term *their* that either Joseph or Jesus needed to be purified also. Scholars are not sure if both or all three may be included in the term *their*.[20] This may be a subtle hint of equal responsibility for the birthing of the child, Jesus. But the writer chooses not to explore or amplify the joint responsibility at this particular point in the narrative.

Finally Mary and Joseph end their roles together in the narrative during the story about Jesus lingering in Jerusalem during the Passover (Luke 2:41-52). Luke insists that they are a couple by repeatedly calling them parents (Luke 2:41, 44, 48). Together they discover that Jesus is not part of the caravan heading home. Together they travel back to Jerusalem and search for him. Together they find him in the temple dialoguing with the teachers. Luke says that both of them were astonished. Yet it is Mary who speaks. It is Mary who says to her son:

> My son, why have you treated us like this? Your father and I have been searching for you in great anxiety.
> (Luke 2:48, NEB)

She takes the lead in scolding Jesus. They all return home together, and Luke assures the audience that Jesus is under the authority of both of the parents. Neither of the parents understood what had happened in Jerusalem, says Luke (Luke 2:50). Yet Mary seems to understand more than Joseph (Luke 2:51).

Joseph is a lifeless shadow that Luke places at important junctures in the story. He never speaks or gives his opinion. He never lives for the audience. Mary, although neglected in the rest of the gospel, is portrayed as an insightful and self-directed person who is in charge of her life and her family. Her positive response to every circumstance sets a tone for the rest of the gospel. She is part of a couple, a parent. But her distinctive character is obvious to the reader. She is a mother, wife, kinswoman, and friend. Although she serves, Luke never allows the audience to lose sight of this woman's contribution. She does not fade into the background. She is the center of the story.

Women of Independence: Widows

The tears of a pregnant woman touch the heart of Luke as much as the loneliness of a widow. Luke chooses to feature seven stories about widows, taking three of them from Mark. The narratives are life-giving and positive, unlike those of the writer of 1 Timothy who seems to be threatened by the activities of widowed women:

> Moreover, in going round from house to house they [younger widows] learn to be idle, and worse than idle, gossips and busybodies, speaking of things better left unspoken. It is my wish, therefore, that young widows shall marry again . . .   (1 Tim. 5:13, NEB)

Luke makes no such demands upon widows. Their worth, lifestyle, and contributions to the community are cherished. The women do not marry again. Their independence is an asset.

Rather than criticizing widows, Jesus criticizes the

present religious system which seems to place widows in awkward circumstances. Jesus began his itinerate ministry in his hometown, Nazareth, by telling an ancient story about a helpless widow. The problems of widows are well-documented in the ancient Hebrew traditions found in the Hebrew Scriptures (Old Testament). Jesus claimed:

> The spirit of the Lord is upon me because he has anointed me; he has sent me to announce good news to the poor.   (Luke 4:18, NEB)

Who are the poor? Luke begins to answer this question for the audience.

> There were many widows in Israel, you may be sure, in Elijah's time ... yet it was to none of those that Elijah was sent, but to a widow at Sarepta in the territory of Sidon.   (Luke 4:25-27, NEB)

Before a Jewish audience, Jesus boldly tells how God chose to help a non-Jew rather than a Jew, a woman rather than a man.

Elijah, a prophet of the Lord, received word that he should go to Zarephath, a village of Sidon (non-Jewish territory) during an economic recession in Israel. He met a widow and miraculously her store of oil and flour kept multiplying so that she and her son and Elijah did not starve for three years. Subsequently, her son became very ill. Elijah prayed: "O Lord my God, is this thy care for the widow with whom I lodge, that thou hast been so cruel to her son?" (1 Kings 17:21). Her son was restored as a result of that prayer.

Elijah does not appear to be married. Nor does he take a family with him to Sidon. He resides with a non-Jewish widow, who apparently has no other family except her son. They are not married, yet they live as a family. His room was in the attic (1 Kings 17:19). The irony in this story is that Elijah could have helped a Jew—any Jew—but he chose instead to help an outsider.

From the beginning of Jesus' ministry until the bitter end, Luke tells stories that portray Jesus exposing the underside of Hebrew social history. The poor and socially neglected are the ones that are highlighted. Their lives are cherished and discussed. Their stories are important to the community.

Widows who were not poor, often found themselves completely devastated financially after the death of their husbands. Taking a cue from Mark, Luke preserves this caustic appraisal of the religious scribes in Jerusalem in the following condemnation:

> These are the men who eat up the property of widows, while they say long prayers for appearance' sake.   (Luke 20:47; Mark 12:40, NEB)

Not all widows were poor, destitute, or dependent upon their families and religious community for help. Some became vulnerable to religious tactics of the unscrupulous and greedy leaders.

No economic details are given about the widow who lived in Nain. Jesus had left Capernaum and he apparently stumbled into a funeral procession outside the gates of this city. A child lay dead. Luke explains that this child was the only son of the mother.

> The dead man was the only [begotten] son of his
> widowed mother; and many of the townspeople were
> there with her. When the Lord saw her his heart went
> out to her, and he said, "Weep no more."
>
> (Luke 7:12-13, NEB)

Only begotten here is a term that, over the past 2,000
years, has been regularly assigned to Jesus. It is normally
defined as "unique" (John 3:16). But Luke sees this
"uniqueness" in every child and proceeds to tell two more
stories about children who need help and receive it (Luke
8:42; 9:38). Years ago I wrote about Luke's reasons for pre-
serving this story about the widow.

> The widow's predicament is obvious. Her only son
> was dead and about to be buried. In a Jewish society
> the male provided the livelihood for the family. A
> woman was destitute without a man. Luke mentions
> no other family. The woman was left totally alone.
>
> Jesus, upon recognizing her predicament had com-
> passion upon her.... His heart or insides literally
> ached for her....
>
> Jesus could not change the entire cultural status of a
> woman. He could not take away her shame of being
> husbandless, nor her poverty, or loneliness, by
> developing a modern world where she could find new
> life for herself. The only way he could alleviate her
> pain and hopelessness was to provide her with a man.
> And this he did. He gave breath back to her son, and
> with it she regained her life.[21]

After rethinking Luke's reason for the inclusion of this story, it appears to me that the above interpretation does not take into consideration other features of this story, nor Luke's own point of view. Although the man seems to be her only son, she may have had daughters. In any case, she is not alone. The crowd is with her as her son is carried out to be buried.

While my previous interpretation suggests that women cannot successfully live on their own, I now doubt that this was the opinion of Luke himself. Luke records many stories about women who live happy lives without being attached to men. Here, as in the story about the raising of Jairus' daughter, Luke demonstrates Jesus' compassion for the woman and for life itself (Luke 8:49-56). Death is the enemy. Jesus shares her tears and opens his heart to her grief. He stops, touches the "unclean" dead body, risks the sanctions of Judaism, and returns her son to her.[22]

In a very emotional scene Luke says, "His heart went out to her." These are special words for Luke and are used sparingly.[23] Elsewhere they are found only in the stories of the Good Samaritan and the Lost Son (Luke 10:33; 15:20)—and as a noun when speaking about God.

> For in the tender compassion of our God the morning sun from heaven will rise upon us.   (Luke 1:78, NEB)

No other gospel writer displays such emotion and compassion toward people—especially toward women.

This emotional undertone seems to permeate all of Luke's gospel. Jesus weeps for Jerusalem (Luke 19:41) and tells those gathered to listen, that weeping and mourning are part of life.

> How blest are you who weep now; you shall laugh.
> (Luke 6:21, NEB)

> Alas for you who laugh now; you shall mourn and weep.   (Luke 6:25, NEB)

The words *weeping* and *mourning* are used more often by Luke than any other gospel writer.[24] The writer is not afraid to portray the emotional side of people or life. While people weep for the widow's son and for Jairus' only daughter, somehow those tears fade as their perceptions of life and death are changed, their reality reinterpreted by the writer of Luke. Death songs and all their strains give way to the morning sun.

Jesus gives the son over into the safekeeping of his mother. "And Jesus gave him back to his mother" (Luke 7:15). She takes her son. He has come back to her. Her life is not revived. His life is revived. The widow's son's life was a gift. Because of Jesus' compassion, he returned to life. The widow weeps no more.

Luke tells other stories of widows who should weep but do not. The Persistent Widow appears to be a victim of society. She overcomes injustice by her own diligence.

> There was once a judge who cared nothing for God or man, and in the same town there was a widow who constantly came before him demanding justice against her opponent. For a long time he refused; but in the end he said to himself, "True, I care nothing for God or man; but this widow is so great a nuisance that I will see her righted before she wears me out with her persistence."   (Luke 18:2-5, NEB)

While a person may not be in control—may not be part of the powerful—the lesson that Luke teaches is a wise one. Theodore Herzl (or Hertzel), advocate and worker for the Zionist movement who believed that Israel would some day be a nation said, "If you will it, it need not be a dream."[25] According to Coolidge, "Persistence is omnipotent."[26] Luke takes the powerlessness of the poor and turns it into a weapon that has the potential of alleviating the problems and pains of humanity. The writer uses a story about a widow to demonstrate to the community that they must persevere and they will also overcome.

Woman not only overcomes death, disease (cf. the Crippled Woman, Luke 13:10-16), and oppression, she also adds to the community. Her voice signals the dawn of a different kind of day. Anna is one of these women. She is a prophetess. Listen to her story:

> There was also a prophetess, Anna the daughter of Phanuel, of the tribe of Asher. She was a very old woman, who had lived seven years with her husband after she was first married, and then alone as a widow to the age of eighty-four. She never left the temple, but worshipped day and night, fasting and praying. Coming up at that very moment, she returned thanks to God; and she talked about the child to all who were looking for the liberation of Jerusalem.
>
> (Luke 2:36-38, NEB)

Anna is a widow. Apparently she has chosen not to remarry. She makes her home in the temple. Historically this was impossible. Women were segregated to the women's court and during their menstrual period were not allowed to come near to the temple.[27] Her heritage stems from the ancient tribe of Asher in northern Israel (Gen. 49:20-21; Deut. 33:23-24) known for producing wives for the temple priests.[28]

Mary and Joseph meet Anna as they enter the temple in order to present Jesus. It is odd that they are not met by a priest or any official of the temple. Instead they are greeted by an old man named Simeon who has wandered into the temple—and then Anna. Luke does not give the background of Simeon. He may not even be a Jew. He is from Jerusalem waiting for the consolation of Israel.[29] Luke says that he is righteous, devout, and that the Holy Spirit is upon him (Luke 2:25). For some reason he is allowed to hold the baby (Luke 2:27). No reason is given as to why he would be able to do this. He only speaks with Mary, although his prophecies include both Jesus and Joseph (Luke 2:34).

Simeon's speech, like Anna's, is prophetic. He predicts the future for Jesus. He will be a deliverer (Luke 2:29-32). But he predicts disaster for Mary, her life will be fragmented.[30]

> This child is destined to be a sign which men reject; and you too shall be pierced to the heart.
>
> (Luke 2:35, NEB)

Anna also speaks. According to Luke,

> She gave thanks to God and spoke about the child to all who were looking forward to the redemption of Jerusalem.   (Luke 2:38, NIV)

She is called "prophetess" (Luke 2:36). This noun is used only here by Luke and then again by the writer of the book of Revelation (Rev. 2:20). Although women do prophesy in Corinth (1 Cor. 11) and within the stories of Acts (2:17; 21:9), one scholar believes that the title and the office never belonged to women in ancient times.

> Though some women had the spirit of prophesy they were not given this title. There was obvious hesitation to ascribe the title "prophetess" to women.[31]

Luke affirms women as prophetesses and hints that they may be performing priestly functions. Both Simeon and Anna's words reflect those of the ancient prophet Isaiah.

> The Lord has taken pity on his people and has ransomed Jerusalem.   (Isa. 52:9, NEB)

Simeon looks for comfort or pity; Anna looks for redemption, or a ransoming. What more would anyone ask from a priest? What more could an ancient Hebrew priest do for the people? They offer hope for liberation and peace.

In summary, Anna, the widow, prophesies and tells all about Jesus. Simeon, the unknown, peers into the future. Simeon is "righteous" but Anna's dedication to her God is unfathomable. She lives out her religious ideals constantly as she fasts and prays.[32]

Other Widows

Luke's sensitive portrait of widows includes two additional stories taken from Mark which emphasize the equality of widows and their generosity. The first story is about a woman who was widowed seven times (Luke 20:27-40; Mark 12:18-27; Matt. 22:23-33).

This hearty woman survived seven brothers. According to levirate law, each brother was responsible to marry the widow of the deceased brother and to produce a son after the death of a brother.[33] The key question and answer session of this story is as follows:

> "At the resurrection whose wife is she to be, since all seven had married her?" Jesus said to them, "The men and women of this world marry, but those who have been judged worthy of a place in the other world and of the resurrection from the dead, do not marry, for they are not subject to death any longer. They are like angels; they are sons of God, because they share in the resurrection." (Luke 20:33-36, NEB)

The most significant change that Luke makes to the story is the addition of the phrase "sons of God" (Luke 20:36). In the gospel these words are usually used as a title for Jesus (Luke 1:35; 4:3, 9, 41; 8:28; 9:35; 22:70). Only here does Luke use the plural form, "sons of God." By doing this Luke highlights Mark's view of an equal world. Like Jesus who is traced back to Adam, who is of God (Luke 3:38), in the resurrection all will live out their lives in a similar pattern—like the angels. All are children of God from the same family. None will be treated differently. All are co-partners in the world to come.[34]

Equality *in theory* is not the same as equality in reality. Some widows who should be treated equally seem to be victims of society. Yet Luke casts these widows as the leading players in the Jesus story. The story of the poor widow

who gives all (Luke 21:1-4; Mark 12:40-44) remains virtually unchanged. She is a symbol to the community of a
person who lives in a self-sacrificial manner. While life can
be difficult for the widow, Luke reminds the community
not to continue its oppressive tendencies. Here he follows
the thinking of another great writer of long ago, Isaiah:

> Cease to do evil and learn to do right ... champion
> the oppressed, give the orphan his rights, plead the
> widow's cause.   (Isa. 1:17, NEB)

For Luke, widows seem to be able to take care of themselves. They are astute in their perceptions of religious
traditions and ideals. They overcome, at times, with the
touch of Jesus. At other times they overcome by their own
endurance and persistent determination. Luke does not
weep for the widow. The writer dances and their stories are
remembered.

Women of Independence: Singles

None of the synoptic writers advocates one particular
lifestyle for anyone, especially women. More than any
other synoptic writer, Luke writes stories about women
who choose alternate lifestyles and seem to be independent
and financially astute. Their stories are intermingled
among the many adventures of Jesus. They become friends
and companions within this early Christian community.

In contrast to the many commentators (and some early
church writers) that blame Eve for all the problems of humanity, no gospel portrays women as a temptation for
Jesus.[35] The ancient Hebrews tell a story of temptation in
Genesis that results in both Adam and Eve being escorted

out of the garden (Gen. 2—4). They are left with little more
than animal skins to cover their bodies. Jesus faces no such
temptation. In the play, *Jesus Christ Superstar,* Mary sings
a song about loving Jesus.[36] The composer hints at a special
relationship between the two. The rest of the New
Testament has virtually nothing to say about this relationship. Yet later Christian writings tell stories about Mary
Magdalene and Jesus. They claim that Jesus gave her more
attention than the twelve—that seeming rivalry and
jealousy broke out as the disciples competed for the attention of Jesus.[37]

While the gospels do not hint that Jesus had a love affair
or was deceived by a woman, Luke does claim that some
women were very close friends of Jesus. From the conversation of Mary with Gabriel (Luke 1:26-28) to the resurrection, women walk and talk with Jesus. They are never a
problem, nor do they treat people in an abusive manner.
They are part of the solid foundation of Luke's view of this
early Christian community.

Luke presents a balanced view on woman and childbearing and rearing. Mothers and singles are important to
the community.[38] Two verses or stories illustrate this: Elizabeth declares at the conception of John, "Now at last he
has deigned to take away my reproach among men" (Luke
1:25, NEB). Yet later the writer chooses to include these
sayings:

> Daughters of Jerusalem, do not weep for me; no,
> weep for yourselves and your children. For the days
> are surely coming when they will say, "Happy are the
> barren, the wombs that never bore a child, the breasts
> that never fed one."[39]   (Luke 23:28-29, NEB)

As Jesus was saying these things, a woman in the crowd called out, "Blessed is the mother who gave you birth and nursed you!" He replied, "Blessed rather are those who hear the word of God and obey it."　　　　　　　　　　　　　(Luke 11:27-28, NIV)

Both of the above quotations reflect a time of violence in the life of the writer.[40] The most recent known violence was the destruction of Jerusalem by the Romans in A.D. 70. After the fall of Jerusalem, life for the Jew—and even the Gentile—had to be different. Life was no longer solid like the huge stone walls of the temple. There was no promise of tomorrow. Perhaps many would say to themselves that they would rather be dead than face the rebuilding of their fire-scorched lands, broken homes, and families.

Wherever Luke's community was located in the Roman Empire,[41] the writer remembered times when children were a liability, not a blessing, and the strength of a woman was not in her childbearing or childrearing capacities. Elisabeth Schüssler Fiorenza says, "Faithful discipleship, not biological motherhood, is the eschatological calling of women."[42]

The above laments serve to remind the congregation of the not-so-distant past. The Jewish people had experienced war after war. They knew its desolating impact on their lives. When Luke says, "Blessed are the barren" (Luke 23:29), the writer may be recalling other violent times. Jeremiah and Isaiah both have similar sayings about women and childbearing.

Let their women be childless and widowed, let death

> carry off their men, let their young men be cut down
> in battle.   (Jer. 18:21, NEB)

> Sing aloud, O barren woman who never bore a child,
> break into cries of joy, you who have never been in
> labor.   (Isa. 54:1-2, NEB)

Similarly Luke preserves this phrase from the gospel of Mark:

> Alas for women who are with child in those days, or
> have children at the breast.
>   (Mark 13:17; Luke 21:23; Matt. 24:19, NEB)

Childbearing, according to Luke, should be done during times of peace. The wiser woman—the woman who has experienced the pain of the wars—will bear no children.[43]

Yet married women, according to Luke, followed Jesus and kept company with the twelve (Luke 8:1-3).[44] Children are never mentioned in conjunction with them. These women made the choice to follow Jesus, unlike the young man who said,

> I have just got married and for that reason I cannot
> come.   (Luke 14:20, NEB)

Luke says they financed Jesus' itinerant ministry.[45] Listen to this story:

> After this he went journeying from town to town and
> village to village, proclaiming the good news of the
> kingdom of God. With him were the Twelve and a

number of women who had been set free from evil
spirits and infirmities: Mary, known as Mary of Magdala, from whom seven devils had come out, Joanna,
the wife of Chuza a steward of Herod's, Susanna, and
many others [women]. These women provided for
them out of their own resources.[46]   (Luke 8:1-3, NEB)

Together with the twelve, these women were more than
companions for Jesus. Their personal identities and names
are lost forever. Yet Luke identifies them as essential in-
gredients in Jesus' itinerant ministry. They are part of the
group "with him" (Luke 8:1-3). J. Massyngberde-Ford
concludes that they were disciples.[47] Luke may be hinting
that they were affluent women. There is ample evidence
throughout the history of the church to support such an
idea,[48] although E. Moltmann-Wendel believes that
Joanna had a political background and questions whether
women would fit into the ideal of Lucan discipleship and
poverty.

The sayings of Jesus handed down by Luke do not fit
well with women like Mary Magdalene, Joanna, and
Susanna, who have possessions: "Sell your goods and
give the money to the poor. . . . No one can be my
disciple unless he gives up everything. . . ."[49]

Moltmann-Wendel has missed the thrust of Luke's reasons
for including this story about the traveling women. They
are doing precisely what the writer would want them to do.
Aren't they sharing of themselves and their properties?
Haven't they given all to follow Jesus?

Traditional commentaries interpret the phrase "provided for them out of their own resources" (Luke 8:3, NEB) as service in the area of menial labor. According to Ben Witherington III,

> Being Jesus' disciples did not lead these women to abandon their traditional roles in regard to preparing food, serving, etc.[50]

Some have suggested that they followed Jesus because they were the wives of the twelve.[51] Yet manuscript evidence suggests that their donations and duties could have been solely for Jesus.[52]

Whether or not they were sharing with Jesus or others, the point is that they were *sharing*. They mirror Luke's idealism about the history of the early Christian communities found in Acts.[53]

> All whose faith had drawn them together held everything in common: they would sell their property and possessions and make a general distribution as the need of each required.   (Acts 2:44-45, NEB)

In summary, Luke told stories about independent women who may have been wealthy. They chose to share of themselves and their possessions.

Another story preserved by Luke (taken from Mark) demonstrates Luke's loyalty to women who are financially astute. In the story about the Woman Who Touched Jesus,[54] Luke omits this phrase which deals with the woman's resources.

> In spite of long treatment by many doctors, on which

she had spent all she had, there had been no improve-
ment; on the contrary, she had grown worse.

(Mark 5:26, NEB)

Luke does not center the story around the woman's personal dilemma (Luke 8:43). Nor does the writer suggest
that she is destitute. She comes to Jesus, not as a penniless
woman, but as a woman who has tried every other alternative.

Independent women are part of the heart of the gospel.
Luke continues this theme by telling two stories about
single women who are single-mindedly dedicated to their
religious beliefs. Included in the discussion are stories
about Martha and her sister Mary, the Woman Who Loves
Jesus.

The following story—not found in Matthew or Mark—is
about two sisters who choose different lifestyles within the
community of Jesus.

> While they were on their way Jesus came to a village
> where a woman named Martha made him welcome in
> her home. She had a sister, Mary, who seated herself
> at the Lord's feet and stayed there listening to his
> words. Now Martha was distracted by her many tasks,
> so she came to him and said, "Lord, do you not care
> that my sister has left me to get on with the work by
> myself? Tell her to come and lend a hand." But the
> Lord answered, "Martha, Martha, you are fretting
> and fussing about so many things; but one thing is
> necessary. The part that Mary has chosen is best; and
> it shall not be taken away from her."
>
> (Luke 10:38-42, NEB)

In recent years, commentaries and books on women have continued to interpret this story against the background of Judaism. They conclude that the Jesus in Luke is breaking long-held Jewish traditions. Jesus talks with a woman, eats with a woman, teaches a woman, and finally is served by a woman.[55] These were not normal Jewish practices for Jewish men during the time of Jesus.[56] Yet Luke is attempting to relate more than the breaking of taboos. Luke is attempting to solve a dilemma faced by women by opening up the future for both the Marys and Marthas of the next generation. The issue in this story is service—two types of service.

Martha owns the house. She seems to be running it. According to Richard J. Dillon, Martha—like Zacchaeus—may have housed itinerant preachers.[57] In Luke the beginnings of Christian gatherings are often found in the homes of people who shared a common commitment.[58] Scholars today call these house churches.[59] It is believed that they served as communal meeting places until worship became safe and tolerable. Later people moved into larger buildings.[60] Over forty years ago, Floyd Filson wrote:

> It thus appears that the house church was a vital factor in the church's development during the first century, and even in later generations. It provided the setting in which the primitive Christians achieved a mental separation from Judaism before the actual break occurred. . . . It explains in part the proneness of the apostolic church to divide. It helps us gain a true understanding of the influential place of families of means in what has been sometimes been regarded as church of the dispossessed.[61]

Perhaps the writer of Luke intends the readers to understand Martha's home to be one of those outposts that took care of people. According to Fiorenza, "Traveling missionaries and house churches were central to the Christian mission which depended upon mobility and patronage and women were leaders in both areas."[62] If this is a story about a house church, then the dilemma is not over serving tables but over what type of service is most important for the person and the community. Luke uses the term *serve* in much the same manner as Mark. Woman, service, and Jesus are connected as Jesus says, "Yet here am I among you like a servant" (Luke 22:27; see also 4:39; 8:3; 10:40; 12:37; 17:8).

The dilemma in the community could be stated this way: Should followers of Jesus be itinerants who own no land nor carry any possession? or should they own their own property and share it with others? Luke recorded rigid ascetic goals earlier in the gospel story:

> Carry no purse or pack, and travel barefoot. Exchange no greetings on the road. (Luke 10:5, NEB)

> "Take nothing for the journey," he told them, "neither stick nor pack, neither bread nor money; nor are you each to have a second coat. When you are admitted to a house, stay there, and go on from there."
> (Luke 9:3-4, NEB)

D. W. Riddle suggests that in early Christian communities both bishops and widows housed itinerants and served as examples of hospitality to the community.[63]

While Martha is busy, Mary sits at the feet of Jesus and

learns. According to Luke, Mary has chosen a better way.[64] She is like one of the students of the ancient philosophers. She follows her teacher. She is freed from the sometimes tedious responsibilities of home ownership. Nor is she encumbered with administrative tasks related to a house church. Luke asserts that the best way is the way of the women found in Luke 8:1-3. People who choose the life of the itinerant reflective lifestyle may be happier than those who own a home. The life of the engaged thinker is preferred to the sedentary life.[65] Both are necessary in the building of the community.

Mary and Martha are women. Therefore it has been assumed that the issue of this story is domestic.[66] If the setting is a house church then very different conclusions can be drawn. For Luke, women are very important to the community. They serve in at least two key positions. They have a choice of vocations, neither of which revolve around a married homelife. These women are women of independent means who have futures within the community that meets in the name of Jesus.

Another independent woman that Luke chooses to study is the Loving Woman (Luke 7:3-50). Although this story is similar to the stories found in Matthew and Mark, scholars generally conclude that it finds its origin in a separate tradition.[67]

The usual or customary title for this story is "The Sinful Woman." This title would lead the reader to imagine all sorts of things about the woman's character.[68] *The New English Bible* translates the beginning verse of this story, "A woman who was living an immoral life." The *New International Version* translates it, "A woman who lived a sinful life," and the *Revised Standard Version* more correctly translates it, "A woman of the city, who was a sinner." Several traditional and more recent works would agree with this statement made by Jewett:[69]

> She was evidently a prostitute who had been redeemed through the ministry of Jesus, perhaps the first man who had ever treated her as a person rather than a sex object.[70]

The above interpretation is both patronizing and inaccurate. The writer assumes that the woman is a prostitute, based upon the word *sinner* and (perhaps) the scene which describes her letting down her hair.[71] But if one studies the word *sinner* in the context of Luke, one discovers that many people are called "sinners." Among the most obvious are Peter and Zacchaeus (Luke 5:8; 19:7), yet no one would ever call Peter a prostitute. Sinners eat with Jesus (Luke 5:30-31; 19:7), they crowd close to hear Jesus (Luke 15:1), and are said to be generous and loving people (Luke 6:32-34).

Jesus is often accused of being a friend of tax collectors and sinners (Luke 15:2) and in one verse the allegations reach a "fever pitch":

> "Look at him! a glutton and a drinker, a friend of tax-gatherers and sinners."   (Luke 7:34, NEB)

In an almost sarcastic fashion, Jesus answers the Pharisees:

> "It is not the healthy that need a doctor, but the sick; I have not come to invite virtuous people, but to call sinners to repentance."   (Luke 5:31-32, NEB)

Jesus makes no apologies for his company, nor does he look down upon people termed "sinners." They are his equals. According to Fiorenza the term *sinners* represented everything from fruit-sellers and bartenders to any job that had "service" as its goal.[72] Listen to the story of the Loving Woman as told by Luke:

> Now one of the Pharisees invited Jesus to have dinner with him, so he went to the Pharisee's house and reclined at the table. When a woman who had lived a sinful life in that town learned that Jesus was eating at the Pharisee's house, she brought an alabaster jar of perfume, and as she stood behind him at his feet weeping, she began to wet his feet with her tears. Then she wiped them with her hair, kissed them and poured perfume on them.

> When the Pharisee who had invited him saw this, he said to himself, "If this man were a prophet, he would know who is touching him and what kind of woman she is—that she is a sinner." Jesus answered him . . . .

> Then he turned toward the woman and said to Simon, "Do you see this woman? I came into your house. You did not give me any water for my feet, but she wet my feet with her tears and wiped them with her hair. You did not give me a kiss, but this woman, from the time I entered, has not stopped kissing my feet. You did not put oil on my head, but she has poured perfume on my feet. Therefore, I tell you, her many sins have been forgiven—for she loved much. But he who has been forgiven little loves little."

Then Jesus said to her, "Your sins are forgiven."

The other guests began to say among themselves, "Who is this who even forgives sins?"

Jesus said to the woman, "Your faith has saved you; go in peace."   (Luke 7:36-50, NIV)

It was Jesus' practice, according to Luke, to eat with Pharisees (Luke 7:36; 11:37; 14:1) and dialogue with them about religious issues (Luke 5:17, 21, 30, 33; 6:2; 11:38-39; 15:2; 17:20; 19:39). Although they listen to him (Luke 5:17), Jesus still "insults" them.

Woe to you Pharisees, because you love the most important seats in the synagogues and greetings in the marketplaces.   (Luke 11:43, NIV)

Woe to you Pharisees, because you give God a tenth of your mint, rue and all other kinds of garden herbs, but you neglect justice and the love of God.
                        (Luke 11:42, NIV)

The Pharisees seem to be very close to Jesus, but they do not believe his words. They are not part of those that follow him. Although they eat with Jesus they do not seem to share anything with anyone. The disciples are always set apart from them (Luke 19:39). The Pharisees are pious people (Luke 18:10-11) who love money and are stingy (Luke 16:14), according to Luke.

The word *love* is used in connection with the Pharisees only twice in Luke's work. They love their political powers and neglect the love of God (Luke 11:42-43). Contrarily, Luke portrays the Loving Woman as an opposite to the Pharisees. She is humble. She gives. She shares of her belongings. She exhibits care and emotion for Jesus and herself. She loves.

Rarely does Luke use the term *kiss* as a noun or a verb (Luke 15:20; 22:48). Here the woman touches Jesus with her lips. The only other character to do this is Judas (Luke 22:48). Her relationship with Jesus is distinct. It is familiar, close, emotional, caring, and attentive.

Both Q. Quesnell and R. J. Dillon see this woman as a follower of Jesus and part of his table company.[73] Like no one else in any of Luke's writings, she "loved much" (Luke 7:47). Although she is alone, she knows how to give both her material goods and herself. Jesus receives her gifts.[74]

Like Mary who sat at the feet of Jesus, Jesus now sits at the feet of this woman. It is similar to the story found in the gospel of John where Jesus begins to wash the feet of the disciples in order to teach them love and humility (John 13:1-17). For Luke it is the woman who silently and carefully ministers.[75] According to M. C. Detrick, "The woman did not quietly ask permission, but she acted on her own authority."[76] She asks nothing from Jesus. She only gives. Her reward stems from her own self-confidence and faith. "Your faith has saved you" (Luke 7:50).

This ends the discussion of the Lucan stories about independent and resourceful women. Luke does not isolate women. The writer preserves stories that must have been cherished. They are about daring women who, in spite of their circumstances, had the courage to choose and live out their own lifestyles. We will now explore Luke's view of traditions that highlight partnership rather than independence.

Partnership and Friendship

According to Mary Daly, partnership between woman and man can never be a solution to the "woman problem" facing our society today. Instead, she proposes a female revolution. For her, the key to winning equality is first isolation, next, creation of a new world, and then domination.

> The radical be-ing of women is very much an otherworld journey. It is both discovery and creation of a world other than Patriarchy.[77]

Contrarily, Luke isolates neither woman nor man. Nor does the writer claim dominance for woman or man in administrative matters in the early community. They walk side by side in their journeyings.[78]

Luke remembers stories about both sexes. This selection of material which results in a "communal" vocabulary seeks to unite people rather than to separate. It allows the audience to see both sexes as part of the story about Jesus. Consequently the writer adds traditions that seem to break the myth of the all-male following of Jesus (1 Cor. 15). People are sent out two by two (Luke 10). Luke is not concerned with their names or their sex. In reading the story about the two on the road to Emmaus (Luke 24), Luke never clearly reveals their identity. One is called Cleopas and we have no name for the other. Are they a couple going home? Or are they two men or two women heading back to their lodging? The following discussion will explore Luke's view of partnership by drawing attention to pairing traditions, friends, couples, and Luke's communal vocabulary.

Pairing Traditions

Luke often matches traditions. If the writer tells a story about a man, immediately following will be a story about a woman or vice versa. According to Constance Parvey,

> Luke not only incorporates some of the "pairing" parables shared by Matthew and Mark but he adds several of his own.[79]

Here are some of the pairs.

Women	Men
Widow of Nain 7:11-17	The Centurion's Slave 7:2-10
Mary and Martha 10:38-42	Good Samaritan 10:29-37
Woman and the Lost Coin 15:8-10	Man with the Lost Sheep 15:3-7
Crippled Woman 13:10-16	Man with Dropsy 14:2-6
Two Women Grinding 17:35	Two Men in Bed 17:34-35
Widow of Zarephath 4:25-26	Naaman the Leper 4:27
The Loving Woman 7:37-50	Simon the Pharisee 7:36-50
The Hemorrhaging Woman 8:43-48	Jairus 8:41-42, 49-56
Queen of the South 11:31	Men of Nineveh 11:32
Widow 18:2-8	Tax Collector 18:10-14
Daughters of Jerusalem 23:28	Simon of Cyrene 23:26[80]

Male-female pairing is not the only partnership device used by Luke. Women and women, men and men, and women and men become friends and companions in the Lucan drama. Note these pairs: Mary and Martha (Luke 10:38-42), Herod and Herodias (Luke 3:18-20), James and John (Luke 5:10), Mary and Joseph (Luke 1—3), Simeon and Anna (Luke 2:22-38), and Elizabeth and Zechariah (Luke 1). In these stories Luke emphasizes individuality plus companionship—the sharing of life with another person. This sharing of life is most noticeable in the "communal" vocabulary employed by Luke. Of all the synoptic writers, Luke has the most diverse vocabulary when it comes to describing personal relationships.

Friends and Acquaintances

Luke is fond of using the word *friend.* Matthew uses the term only once, and Mark omits it. According to *The Random House Dictionary*, a friend is:

> a person attached to another person by feelings of affection or personal regard,
> a patron or a supporter,
> a person who is not hostile (acquaintance, companion, comrade).[81]

Indeed, even in ancient times the word *friend* was a special term for a close association with a loved one, a favorite, or even an ally. It often had political ramifications.[82]

For Luke the word *friend* is almost magical. Luke is the only writer to include a parable about a friend (Luke 11:5-8) and to tell the audience that Herod and Pilate became friends (Luke 23:12). All types of people become friends and share joys and intimacies together in the Lucan story.

Celebrations with friends occur after a lost sheep and a coin are found (Luke 15:6-9). The woman who finds her lost coin calls her woman-friends to celebrate with her.[83] The shepherd calls his male companions and they do the same. The brother of the prodigal son laments to his father, "You never gave me even a young goat so I could celebrate with my friends" (Luke 15:29, NIV). Not only is family invited to huge parties, so are friends (Luke 16:9).

Like the closest of family, friends may betray one (Luke 21:16). Yet Luke's obvious opinion is that friends are an asset and they are certainly worth pursuing. Jesus calls the disciples his friends (Luke 12:1-4) and claims that Jesus was a friend to tax collectors and sinners (Luke 7:34).

The idea of friendship as close companionship is supported by other Lucan words which suggest that a close bond can be made between people. This bond does not have to be based upon a family bloodline. Luke seems to be aware of the "other" and "one another" more than any other gospel.[84] *Other* is used 33 times by Luke and *one another* is used twice as often when compared with the other Synoptics. In all but two instances, the word *one another* is used in the context of speaking with someone else (Luke 12:1; 23:12). For Luke, it is important for people to discuss things with each other and find answers to their problems (e.g., Luke 2:15; 4:36; 6:11; 8:25).

Along with this emphasis on friendship and discussion with one another, Luke adds words that imply a closeness. There are people with Jesus. Some of these people are called "partners" (Luke 5:7, 10), "sharers" (Luke 5:10), "acquaintances" (Luke 2:44), and "company" (Luke 2:44). While Luke does not use the word *two* as often as Mark, the writer does enjoy using the term *both* (Luke 1:6, 7; 5:7; 6:39; 7:42). For instance in the story of Zechariah and Elizabeth "both" are termed blameless (Luke 1:6). In the parable of two men who owed money to a moneylender, "both" men received cancellation of their debts (Luke 7:42). Operations within the community should not be a single-minded affair. In order to make a community what it should be, according to Luke, it takes cooperation between friends and people of both sexes.

This emphasis upon friendship by Luke is not at the expense of a family tradition. The stories of the births of John and Jesus are strong evidence of this. Yet Luke adds words to the gospel that are not used by the other Synoptics. In addition to regular family members, Luke adds the word *kinsperson* (Luke 1:36, 58, 61; 14:12; 21:16), denoting a special family member. Not only are members of the family special, so are the neighbors and the neighborhood people (Luke 1:58; 4:14; 10:27, 29, 36).

Together at the Empty Tomb

Elisabeth Schüssler Fiorenza in her recent book, *In Memory of Her*, says this about the writer of Luke:

> Luke's conception of history is harmonizing and therefore does not acknowledge a "woman's" problem in the early church.[85]

According to Fiorenza, "Luke gives the impression that the leadership of the early Christian mission was totally in the hands of men."[86] However if one studies closely the narratives about the witnesses of Jesus' death and resurrection, one does not find this pattern. Like Matthew, Luke tells a story about fully informed women who witnessed the empty tomb of Jesus and became able participants in this revelatory activity.

As usual, the events in Luke are rearranged and names are different than those in Mark. According to R. J. Dillon, "The names we encounter now are in agreement with no previous listing, neither Mark's nor Luke's own of 8:2f."[87]

Unlike Mark and Matthew, Luke's gospel includes men in the group of people watching Jesus die—all those who knew him" (Luke 23:49, NIV). Even though men are present they do not follow the women to the tomb. Only Joseph and the women know the circumstances of the burial (Luke 23:55). The following Lucan interpretation of the story rehearses an account of the first witnesses of the empty tomb:

> But on the first day of the week, at early dawn, they went to the tomb, taking the spices which they had prepared. And they found the stone rolled away from the tomb, but when they went in they did not find the body. While they were perplexed about this, behold, two men stood by them in dazzling apparel; and as they were frightened and bowed their faces to the ground, the men said to them, "Why do you seek the living among the dead? Remember how he told you, while he was still in Galilee, that the Son of man must be delivered into the hands of sinful men, and be crucified, and on the third day rise. And they remembered his words, and returning from the tomb they told all this to the eleven and to all the rest. Now it was Mary Magdalene and Joanna and Mary the mother of James and the other women with them who

told this to the apostles; but these words seemed to
them an idle tale, and they did not believe them.
(Luke 24:1-11, RSV)

The women remember Jesus' words. They understand
the implication of the empty tomb. They do not need to be
told directly by the resurrected Jesus (Luke 24:4, 45). The
eleven and the others do not believe them.[88] While some
may interpret this as a negative statement about the
women, it is really a negative statement about the eleven.

The problem is not with the women, but with the eleven
and the rest. Their faith and comprehension of Jesus was so
weak that they did not or could not believe the women.
(Perhaps this is an early feminist critique of a society that
rarely accepted the opinion or testimony of a woman.)[89] It
is at least a criticism by Luke of those who in the next verse
are called apostles.[90] Even Peter, after witnessing and veri-
fying the empty tomb, does not believe; he only wonders
(Luke 24:12).[91]

The two on the road to Emmaus do not understand or
see Jesus until they experience the miracle of the breaking
of the bread (Luke 24:30). According to Dillon, the stories
about both the Emmaus travelers and Peter "describe men
under the spell of the messianic *mysterium*, stunned by the
effects of decisive action yet unable to grasp the meaning."[92] Later, after Jesus tells them the story, they remember. He *causes* them to remember (Luke 24:45). No such
miracle is needed for the women.

The women do not need to be told that they should be
witnesses (Luke 24:9). They simply reported their findings.
Luke does not repeat the Marcan statement "they said
nothing to any one, for they were afraid" (Mark 16:8).[93]

Their report was authentic. In every instance that the word *report* is used by Luke, no one ever questions the conclusions of the reporter (Luke 7:18, 22; 8:20, 34, 36, 47; 9:36; 13:1; 14:21; 18:37; 24:9) like the eleven question the women. In the story about the Hemorrhaging Woman, Jesus accepts her report as authentic (Luke 8:47). No questions are asked.

The women in Luke succeed. In Matthew the women are not faced with this communication problem. Luke seems to heighten the belief and witness problem of the eleven, the apostles. Their perception and memory can only be jogged by a miracle—a supernatural event by Jesus himself. The empty tomb and the reminder of the two men are enough for the women. Together the women and the men are presented with the worldwide challenge.

> Begin from Jerusalem, it is you who are the witnesses to it all. And mark this: I am sending upon you my Father's promised gift....   (Luke 24:48-49, NEB)

Together they find Jesus in the breaking of the bread. Together they begin the story of the foundation of early Christianity (Acts 1—2). Both sexes find in themselves distinctive ministries that benefit all. The time and the occasion are the only notable differences.

Summary

Luke remembers stories that appreciate a variety of lifestyles for women. The writer offers no absolute solutions or patterns for correct living as do some of the other New Testament writers. Life for women was demanding and open. They had choices to make. Life was not easy in those days. They could overcome and find success. No matter what their choice, their vocation, their status, their emotional or physical state, they knew they would certainly be called "daughter" by Jesus.

4

Reflections on My Conversations with Mark, Matthew, and Luke

*I met
three seekers
from the other side
of time*

*we talked
we laughed
we sang a song*

*it seemed as if
the waters parted for us.*

All three gospel writers faced a world not unlike our own. Technological and military advances meant that it was generally safe for the average person to travel throughout the Near East. Roman roads were so well-engineered that they eventually became foundations for modern highways from Egypt to Great Britain. Aqueducts carried water to all of the major cities of the Roman Empire. People were traveling more and buying all sorts of foreign goods. To be successful in business, a person from a Jewish family would have to be at least bilingual. People worshiped differently and kept a variety of sacred holidays.

Life was changing for everyone. Rome's military might and strong organizational structure was oppressive to some but to others it brought security and a welcomed orderliness in government. With the technological advances, availability of safe travel, and the influx of foreign people and goods, many social problems arose in each gospel writer's community.

Social and religious roles for women were changing. Roman women managed their own estates while Egyptian women inherited all real estate. The worship of the goddess, Isis, began sweeping the empire. It became fashionable to ordain women as goddesses after their deaths. There is even evidence that women participated in the Olympic games during the first century.

Life was not so privileged for many who were born without royal blood, connections, or a substantial inheritance. The average woman found herself lucky to find a man who could provide for her. The ancient world offered few opportunities for employment for women outside of the home. At best she could be bought by a rich slave owner and schooled in letters or medicine. Generally, Jewish women received only minimal tutoring in reading and computing. Depending on where you lived in the empire, a woman might be cloistered most of her life, as in upper Macedonia, or highly involved in the government activities, as in Sparta.

Yet the pressures to change and adjust were great upon

every citizen of the empire. Adding to this difficult situation were the Jewish zealots who were part of a revolt which swept across Palestine. Christians and Jews felt the effects of these rebellions. Thousands were killed or died of starvation. Others were crippled physically and emotionally. Many were forced to begin a new life far away from Palestine after the total annihilation of Jerusalem.

The gospel writers hoped to help people cope with the technological advances and changes that were taking place in their lives. They offer truly remarkable stories about women who chose a variety of creative, traditional, and independent lifestyles in order to become what they had to be in their world.

A Conversation with Mark

Mark's gospel downplays the traditional idea of an all-male following of Jesus (1 Cor. 15:1-6). The gospel contains stories about faithful women whose strength is exhibited in many different ways. Yet the writer affirms the traditional role of service to others. Giving of oneself for the benefit of someone else is one of the writer's highest ideals. Jesus and the women exemplified this ideal.

Many modern women feel most comfortable in a subordinate or service-type position. As mentioned earlier, feminists criticize this tendency of constant personal sacrifice. Women give to the point of no return. They give until there is nothing left of themselves. Some, in their struggle to rekindle their self-esteem, have left behind broken homes, marriages, lost children, and abandoned lives.

Giving to others does not have to result in a loss of identity. Women need to learn how to limit their giving.

Giving to others awakens a familiar spirit between people. It fosters love and wholeness in both parties. How could anyone want to abandon this opportunity? Women should take pride in their caring gifts. Ann Thacher captures a woman's sense of caring in the beginning verses of her poem entitled "The World of Women."

> The world of women
> is a round world.
> Leaning from windows,
> sighing along earth's
> curve in our encirclement,
> we apprehend that
> world in an embrace.[1]

Women need to give but they also need to know when to limit these efforts. Perhaps women today should practice listening to their own minds about choices of giving in their lives. Perhaps, once in a while, they should consider their own desires first.

Women have rarely been monetarily rewarded while fulfilling Mark's ideals of service to others. In our society, people who choose to work in service-oriented or helping positions, such as nurses, nurse aides, secretaries, caretakers of the elderly, preschool teachers, teachers, social workers, are paid some of the lowest professional wages in the country. Day after day we read in the newspaper that women, although liberated, although working at a full-time career, are losing the battle for equal pay and equal recognition. They are far behind their male associates even though they make up over 40 percent of the work force. Society seems to penalize a woman for choosing a career other than child-rearing or home-building.

Mark emphasizes neither of these domestic careers for women. Women are integral parts of the growth of Christianity. There did not seem to be enough time to think about children and homes.

Yet Mark does not advocate celibacy. Mark abhors any laws or social mores that would penalize the sexes from interacting and being together.

Lastly, Mark fosters a sense of personal strength in the readers. It was not the faith of Jesus that healed the Hemorrhaging Woman; it was her faith. She was aggressively involved in the pursuit of someone who might heal her. Mark applauds women who are independent, resourceful, and willing to risk for the sake of themselves or others. They were the leaders of an ancient religious community and are leaders of many communities today.

Health comes from practicing self-love and self-care. One's dreams can come into existence. One only has to continue to persevere.

Rubem Alves speaks of the presence of the absent. To long for something in the future can help it to be present, alive, in everyday moments. Dreaming and hoping will eventually give birth to reality. In his book, *What Is Religion*, Alves attempts to explain humanity's hopes.

> The fact is that human beings refuse to be what animals are—the sum total of what the past offers them. They have become inventors of worlds. And they have planted gardens, made huts, houses and palaces, constructed drums, flutes, and harps, written poems, changed their bodies, covering them with paint, metal, brands, and cloth, invented flags, built altars,

buried their dead and prepared them for travel, and in their absence sung laments for days and nights.

And we ask ourselves about the inspiration for these worlds which men and women have imagined and built, and we are taken by astonishment.[2]

Mark knows that women can dream. Stories are told about their strength of faith. Mark dreams too. Mark hopes for a speedy return of Jesus to Galilee.

A Conversation with Matthew

Matthew's vision of women transcends time. The writer shows that women have been significant contributors to religious communities for centuries. It was not so unusual for God to choose a woman. Women had always known and followed the divine impulse.

Like Matthew, feminists today are rethinking, researching, and rediscovering the contributions of women in the present and past. Daring women have always chosen unorthodox and courageous routes. They have contributed significantly to the welfare and development of individuals, governments, businesses, and religions throughout history. Their deeds are not usually worshiped, but that does not make their contribution any less important.

Sheila Collins attempts to explain why this pursuit is so important to every woman in her article, "Reflections on the Meaning of Herstory."

History, Simon Weil pointed out in *The Need for Roots*, has always been written by the conquerors. To the extent that history represents the world view and value system of those who have "won," it is to that extent a distortion of the totality of reality systems which could be extant at any period of time. . . .

Women's herstory seeks to open up to purview the vast panorama of human experience, so that reality systems may be seen in their relationship to one another. . . .

Herstory focuses light on the hidden assumptions and agreements, the disguised structure of language and emotion, and the cultural biases and accretions which determine the telling of patriarchal history.[3]

Matthew understood the biases within the ancient traditions. With a fresh approach to telling history, Matthew unashamedly names important, contributing women.

Matthew would encourage any woman to make her contribution. Innovators, creators, and stars always make waves. People tend to resist new ideas even if the end result would solve a problem and make them happier. Today's world would be just as shocked as Matthew's if the newspaper reported that a woman had broken the three-minute mile or synthesized a fuel that could catapult a person beyond our galaxy in only a few seconds. Yet both of these may happen.

Our world often belittles the contributions of women. It appears that Matthew's community had similar problems. Matthew shocks the community into an awareness of different lifestyles for women. Mary was not the first unusual woman to have listened to the divine. God chose a woman to bring the Messiah into existence. Matthew applauds the traditional family ideals of child-rearing and home-building. But the writer does not worship them. They can fall apart under extreme pressure. Matthew encourages married people to stay married. But he also encourages the single, the celibate, and the virgin to live out their lives in ways that are appropriate.

While many women have made great contributions to the growth and stabilization of Christianity throughout history, women have only in recent history begun to be accepted as pastors, professors, and religious leaders within the communities. Matthew recognized their strength and talents years ago, but Matthew's idealism was overlooked for centuries.

Matthew's gospel teaches people to be inclusive, not exclusive. Even in denominations or churches that accept women on the surface and ordain them to important positions, there remains a loneliness that haunts the woman who would be different. Phyllis Trible wrote a sermon about the ordination of Mary Beale, entitled "The Opportunity for Loneliness." Here are some excerpts from it.

> Mary Beale is set apart for the ministry in an age when the church stands on the boundary, when it has failed to be true to its meaning under God, when it moves inexorably into exile. And she too will know the loneliness of being set apart. "Why, Mary, you don't look old enough to be a minister," some will say. And Mary will know the loneliness of age. "Why, Mary, you're too pretty to be a clergy*man!*" So runs that ugly compliment which isolates, alienates, and objectifies a human being; the loneliness of beauty intertwined with the loneliness of sex. Mary is set apart

to witness to truth and to freedom in a male bastion
called the church, a bastion none too eager to free itself of the sin of sexism . . . .

Set apart by God who may come in silence or even
enmity.[4]

Jeremiah once wrote,

> I did not sit in the company of
>   merrymakers,
>   nor did I rejoice;
> I sat alone, because thy hand was
>   upon me,
>   for thou hadst filled me with
>   indignation.
> Why is my pain unceasing,
>   my wound incurable,
>   refusing to be healed?

(Jer. 15:17-18, RSV)

Matthew implies that all people should be treated as
family members. Ancient restrictive traditions may have
met the needs of people in the past, but they must give
way to an openness, a changing family relationship in the
future. Without this openness to women—all types of
women—the community will not become all that it can be.
Women can make a significant difference in the quality of
life for everyone.

Matthew recognizes the tenaciousness of women, especially in the story of the foreign woman who wanted Jesus
to heal her daughter. Women today are finding that they

have many challenges and responsibilities. They may have a home, a job, and classes to take at the local college in the evenings. Some of these women may be married, but more and more it is the single woman, the abandoned woman, the divorced or widowed woman who must cope alone with all of the changes. Matthew's stories recognize the strengths of women to succeed.

Finally, Matthew emphasizes flexibility and communal responsibility. People should be peacemakers and care-takers of whomever they meet. Life should be better for those who meet in the name of Jesus within Matthew's community.

A Conversation with Luke

Luke's view of women blazes across the pages of time. Luke not only opens the minds of the readers; Luke challenges the reader to accept radical new lifestyles for women. In a no-nonsense vocabulary Luke appreciatively portrays Jesus' attempts to erase sexist ideas about women. With an inclusive vocabulary and stories about affluent women, innovative women, independent women, Luke presents an almost twentieth-century idealism about the role of women within society.

Women are stars of most of the important stories. Mary and Elizabeth are take-charge mothers who make decisions for themselves from the beginning of the infancy story. Anna predicts the future and functions as a priest figure at the temple when Jesus is presented. Mary and Martha share equally in the foundation careers of women within Christianity. While the Marys may have been preferred by Jesus, it was the Marthas who managed the homes they would have slept in night after night. Affluent women travel with Jesus and monetarily provide for him. Widows receive more space and praise from Luke than any other book in the New Testament. They are bastions of courage and should be respected for their unique, astute decisions and contributions to the community.

The writing of Luke has an aesthetic quality about it. The writer seems to tap into the psyches and emotions of people. Women feel, think, know, love, give, and are loved. Jesus welcomes all types of women freely into his company and companionship.

Luke believes in the intelligence, capabilities, and choices women make for themselves. Luke affirms women of all types of backgrounds and careers. For women today, Luke places no hindrances in their paths. In many ways, Luke would seem to support modern women in all of their pursuits and choices. At the same time, Luke would warn the readers that they should also support women's choices. Whether women are professionals, homemakers, a combination of both, or neither, Luke would say that whatever choice a woman makes should be the best possible choice for her. Women should only be limited by their own dreams. No society, nor Luke's readers, should erect any additional obstacles.

Luke would support both leadership and subordinate roles for women and all the different combinations of these today. Women's generosity can heal an ever-widening range of wounds.

Luke's presentation of women opens doors to exploration. Life does not have to reflect a set of guidelines or preordained lifestyles for any person. It can be an emotionally, aesthetically, and intellectually stimulating journey. James Kavanaugh writes of his personal journey in an introductory poem in his book *There Are Men Too Gentle to Live Among Wolves.*

> I am one of the searchers. There are, I believe millions of us. . . . We continue to explore life, hoping to uncover its ultimate secret. We continue to explore ourselves, hoping to understand. . . .
>
> We searchers are ambitious only for life itself, for everything beautiful it can provide. . . .
>
> This is a book for wanderers, dreamers and lovers, for lonely men and women who dare to ask of life everything good and beautiful. It is for those who are too gentle to live among wolves.[5]

A Roundtable Discussion with the Seekers

In summing up our conversations about women stories in the Synoptics, it appears that the writers agree on many things. They all appreciate the generosity, sensitivity, compassion, love, sacrificial giving, intelligence, and strength of women. Women do not seem to be abusers of others. They share of their material goods without hesitation. Their commitments are genuine and lasting. Even in the face of adversity they keep their promises. They can be initiators and builders and aggressive participants in all types of projects.

They marvel at the jealousy and rivalry expressed toward female followers of Jesus. Most of the stories are about fully informed women who make the appropriate choices for themselves and others. Sometimes men will have to listen to them and their stories because the divine does work with many types of women.

Finally, they all hope for a community where men and women will share ministries equally. They hope for a time when barriers will be broken and the community will experience times of communal joy. This joy would spring forth out of respect and love for each person. Talents will be cultivated and life can be better if we listen and learn to foster talents in each other. The community needs to relax its rigid perceptions of history, law, and the future. Women are a most important part of the future of any community because they know what it means to give, to serve, to have faith, and to succeed.

Women have not only inherited the right to be called "daughters"; they have won it because they were there when all the rest had abandoned Jesus. They are there when we need them, too.

Notes

Introduction

1. Irene Brennan, "Women in the Gospels," *New Blackfriars* 52 (1971), pp. 291-295; Janice Nunnally-Cox, *Foremothers: Women of the Bible* (New York: Seabury Press, 1981); Mary Cline Detrick, "Jesus and Women," *Brethren Life and Thought* 22 (1977):155-161; Alicia C. Faxon, *Women and Jesus* (Philadelphia: United Church Press, 1973); Peter Ketter, *Christ and Womankind,* trans. Isabel McHugh (Maryland: The Newman Press, 1952); Evelyn and Frank Stagg, *Woman in the World of Jesus* (Philadelphia: Westminster Press, 1978); Leonard Swidler, "Jesus was a Feminist," *Southeast Asia Journal of Theology* 13 (1971): 102-110 and most recently *Biblical Affirmations of Woman* (Philadelphia: Westminster Press, 1979); Ben Witherington III, *Jesus and the Ministry of Women: A Study of Jesus' attitude to Women and their Roles as Reflected in his Early Life* (Massachusetts: Cambridge University Press, 1984); Rachel Wahlberg, *Jesus According to a Woman* (New York: Paulist Press, 1975).

2. Georges Barrios, "Women and the Priestly Office according to the Scriptures," *St. Vladimir's Theological Quarterly* 19 (1975): 174-92; Ann McGrew Bennet, "Overcoming the Biblical and Traditional Subordination of Woman," *Radical Religion* 1 (1974): 28-38; J. Massyngberde Ford," *New Blackfriars* 57 (1976): 244-254; Letha Scanzoni and Nancy Hardesty, *All We're Meant to Be: A Biblical Approach to Women's Liberation* (Texas: Word, 1974); Phyllis Trible, "Depatriarchalizing in Biblical Interpretation," *Journal of the American Academy of Religion* 41 (1973): 30-47.

3. Jean Danielou, *Ministry of Women in the Early Church* (London: Faith Press, 1961); J. Massynberde Ford, "Women Leaders in the New Testament," in

Women Priests: A Catholic Commentary on the Vatican Declaration, eds. Leonard and Arlene Swidler (New York: Paulist Press, 1977), pp. 132-134; Elisabeth S. Fiorenza, "The Study of Women in Early Christianity," *Proceedings of the College Theology 1977 Annual Meeting* and "The Apostleship of Women in Early Christianity," in *Woman Priests*, pp. 135-140; Constance F. Parvey, "The Theology and Leadership of Women in the New Testament," in *Religion and Sexism; Images of Women in the Jewish and Christian Traditions*, ed. Rosemary Radford Ruether (New York: Simon and Schuster, 1974), pp. 117-150; Elizabeth M. Tetlow, *Women and Ministry in the New Testament* (New York: Paulist Press, 1980).

4. John H. Hayes and Carl R. Holladay. *Biblical Exegesis: A Beginners Handbook* (Atlanta: John Knox Press, 1982), pp. 20-21.

5. Philip Schaff and Henry Wace. *A Select Library of Nicene and Post Nicene Fathers of the Christian Church.* Second Series. *St. Augustine* (Grand Rapids: William B. Eerdmans, 1956), 6:344.

6. Ibid., *St. Ambrose. Selected Works and Letters Concerning Repentance*, 2:334.

7. For instance, Sean P. Kealy's book *Mark's Gospel: A History of Interpretation* (New York: Paulist Press, 1982) surveys the myriad of interpretations of the Gospel of Mark.

8. For a general introduction to textual criticism see: J. Harold Greenlee. *Scribes, Scrolls, and Scripture. A Student's Guide to New Testament Criticism* (Grand Rapids: William B. Eerdmans, 1985).

9. *The New Oxford Annotated Bible* (1977) and *The New English Bible* (1972) give several possible endings.

10. Hayes and Holladay. *Biblical Exegesis*, pp. 30-41.

11. Rudolph Bultmann. *History of the Synoptic Tradition*, trans. J. Marsh (New York: Harper and Row, 1963).

12. Ibid., pp. 220-240.

13. Ibid., p. 221.

14. Ibid., pp. 220-240.

15. See: Werner Georg Kümmel, *Introduction to the New Testament*, trans. Howard Clark Kee (New York: Abingdon, 1975), pp. 47-48 and B. H. Streeter, *The Four Gospels. A Study of Origins*, rev. ed. (London: The Macmillan Co., 1930).

16. Ibid.

17. Kümmel, *Introduction*, pp. 47-48.

18. Norman Perrin and Dennis Duling, *The New Testament an Introduction. Proclamation and Parenesis, Myth and History.* Second Edition (New York: Harcourt Brace Jovanovich, Inc., 1982), pp. 267-268.

19. Norman Perrin, *What Is Redaction Criticism?* (Philadelphia: Fortress Press, 1969) and Hayes and Holladay, *Biblical Exegesis*, pp. 94-103.

Chapter One

1. Werner Georg Kümmel, *Introduction to the New Testament.* Trans. Howard Clark Kee (New York: Abingdon Press, 1975), pp. 84-95.

2. Sean P. Kealy, *Mark's Gospel: A History of Its Interpretation* (New York: Paulist Press, 1982), pp. 15-16.

3. Ibid., pp. 36-37. See also footnote no. 59.

4. Werner H. Kelber, *The Kingdom in Mark. A New Place and a New Time* (Philadelphia: Fortress Press, 1979); E. H. Lohmeyer, *Galiläa and Jerusalem* (Gottingen: Vandenhoeck and Ruprecht, 1936).

5. Werner Georg Kümmel, *Introduction to the New Testament*, pp. 98-101. Note the references to E. Linneman's work.

6. For a study of the twelve throughout the New Testament see: Elisabeth Schüssler Fiorenza, "The Twelve," in *Women Priests: A Catholic Commentary on the Vatican Declaration*, eds. Arlene and Leonard Swidler (New York: Paulist Press, 1976), pp. 114-122.

7. Theodore J. Weeden, *Mark. Traditions in Conflict (Philadelphia: Fortress Press, 1971), pp. 26-51, and Joseph B. Tyson, "The Blindness of the Disciples in Mark," Journal of Biblical Literature* 80 (1961): 261-268.

8. Ernest Best, "The Twelve in Mark," *Zeitschrift für die Neutestamentliche Wissenschaft* 69 (1978): 11-35.

9. Elizabeth Struthers-Malbon, "Fallible Followers: Women and Men in the Gospel of Mark," *Semeia: The Bible and Feminist Hermeneutics*, 28 (1983): 29-48.

10. See Solomon Zeitlin, *The Rise and Fall of the Judean State*. 3 Vols. (Philadelphia: The Jewish Publication Society of America, 1978).

11. Some scholars view *anathematizein* ("to anathematize or to curse") as reflective. So Peter may be cursing himself. See T. A. Burkill, "Blasphemy. St. Mark's Gospel as Damnation History," in *Christianity, Judaism, and other Greco-Roman Studies for Morton Smith at Sixty*. 2 Vols. ed. J. Neusner (Leiden: E. J. Brill. 1975), I:68.

12. See T. E. Boomershine, "Mark 16:8 and the Apostolic Commission," *Journal of Biblical Literature* 100 (1981): 225-239 for a survey of opinions.

13. David Rhoades and Donald Michie, *Mark as Story: An Introduction to the Narrative of a Gospel* (Philadelphia: Fortress Press, 1982), pp. 129-130.

14. See J. Neusner, "From Scripture to Mishnah. The Origins of the Tractate Niddah," *Journal of Jewish Studies* 39 (1978), 137-148 and the *Idea of Purity in Ancient Judaism* (Leiden: E. J. Brill, 1973). Only the writer of Leviticus and Mark use *en rhusei haimatos* ("flow of blood") (Mark 5:25; Leviticus 15:19-33) and *hē pēge tou haimatos* ("spring of blood") to refer to menstruation (Mark 5:29; Lev. 12:7).

15. Janice Nunnally-Cox, *Foremothers: Women of the Bible* (New York: Seabury Press, 1981), p. 102. See also W. E. Phipps, "The Menstrual Taboo in Judeo-Christian Tradition," *Journal of Religion and Health* 19 (1980): 293-303 and also my article in the *Journal of Biblical Literature*, "Mark 5:24-34 and Leviticus 15. A Reaction to Restrictive Purity Regulations" 103 (1984): 619-623.

16. J. Neusner, "From Scripture to Mishna. The Origins of the Tractate Niddah," *Journal of Jewish Studies* 39 (1978), 137-148 and the *Idea of Purity in Ancient Judaism* (Leiden: E. J. Brill, 1973).

17. Qumran, *CD* 5.6-7; Edward Lohse, *Die Text aus Qumran Hebräisch und*

Deutsch (Germany: Satz und Druck, 1964), pp. 75-76. See also *CD* 4.12 through 5.17.

18. Josephus, *Antiquities*, 3.268; *Jewish Wars*, 5. 227-228; *Against Apion* 2.103-104. See also Philo, *Biblical Antiquities*, 3.8 and *Special Laws*, 3.32-33.

19. Neusner, "From Scripture to Mishnah," 137-148 and S. Berman, "The Status of Women in Halachic Judaism," *Tradition* 14 (1973), 5-27.

20. Leonard Swidler, *Women in Judaism. The Status of Women in Formative Judaism* (New Jersey: Scarecrow Press, 1976), pp. 83-126.

21. J. Duncan M. Derrett, "Mark's Technique. The Hemorrhaging Woman and Jairus' Daughter." *Biblica* 63 (1982) 474-505 sees a prophetic influence here.

22. *Mastix* ("scourge") is only used of Jesus and women in Mark (3:10; 5:29, 34).

23. *Ancilla to the Pre-Socratic Philosophers*. A translation of *Die Fragmente der Vorsokratiker*, Vol. I trans. Kathleen Freeman (Oxford: Basil Blackwell, 1946), p. 28; *Heraclitus, Fragment* 58.

24. John A. Haas, *Annotations on the Gospel According to St. Mark* (New York: The Christian Literature Society, 1895), p. 95; Kiddushin 4.14. See also Alfred Edersheim, *The Life and Times of Jesus the Messiah*, 2 Vols. (New York: Longmans, Green and Co., 1912), I:620.

25. Philip Schaff and Henry Wace, *A Select Library of Nicene and Post-Nicene Fathers of the Christian Church. Saint Chrysostom. Homilies on the Gospel of Matthew* (Grand Rapids: William B. Eerdmans, 1956), 10:207, 205.

26. C. E. B. Cranfield, *The Gospel According to St. Mark. The Cambridge Greek New Testament Commentary* (Cambridge: The University Press, 1959), p. 183.

27. Swidler, *Women in Judaism*, pp. 88-90.

28. Scholars have approached this miracle story from a variety of points of view. Some argue that Jesus did not heal her of his own volition, but that God used Jesus. Early Gnostic writers argued about whether she could have been turned to dust by merely touching Jesus. They see him as a giant energy box ready to burst out with electricity or some type of force at any minute. Others suggest that the woman healed herself without the help of Jesus through autosuggestion or self-hypnosis. Irenaeus, *Against Heresies*, 3.1.2. Walter E. Bundy, *Jesus and the First Three Gospels: An Introduction to the Synoptic Problem* (Cambridge: Harvard University Press, 1955), p. 245.

29. See Rhoades and Michie, *Mark as Story*, pp. 129-130.

30. H. Van Der Loos, *The Miracles of Jesus* (Leiden: E. J. Brill), pp. 509-519.

31. Some think that there were women physicians in Asia Minor. See L. Swidler, "Greco-Roman Feminism and the Reception of the Gospel," in *Traditio-Krisis Renovatio aus Theologischer Sicht*, eds. B. Jaspert and R. Mohr (Marburg: N. G. Elwert, 1976), p. 46.

32. Eusebius. *Ecclesiastical History*. 2 Vols. *The Loeb Classical Library* trans. J. E. Moulton and H. J. Lawlor (New York: Putnams Sons, 1932), II:175-176.

33. *Diakoneō* ("to serve"). *Theological Dictionary of the New Testament*. 1964 ed.

34. See Valerie Saiving's article, "The Human Situation. A Feminine View," in

Womanspirit Rising: A Feminist Reader in Religion (New York: Harper and Row, 1979), pp. 25-42.

35. Ibid., p. 37.

36. R. M. Grant, "War. Just, Holy, Unjust, in Hellenistic and Early Christian Thought," *Augustinianum* 20 (1980), pp. 73-89.

37. *Diakonos* (servant). *Theological Dictionary of the New Testament*. 1964 ed.

38. Howard C. Kee. *Community of the New Age: Studies in Mark's Gospel* (Philadelphia: Westminster Press, 1977), p. 152.

39. Ibid.

40. Matt. 25:42-44.

41. See my article, "And Those Who Followed Feared," *Catholic Biblical Quarterly* 45 (1983): 396-400.

42. Malbon, "Fallible Followers: Women and Men in the Gospel of Mark," pp. 29-48.

43. Kee, *Community of Mark*, p. 149.

44. See Addison G. Wright, "The Widow's Mite: Praise or Lament? A Matter of Context," *Catholic Biblical Quarterly* 44 (1982): 256-265.

45. For a discussion of Matthew's treatment and comparison of these stories, see Janice Capel Anderson, "Matthew, Gender and Reading," in *Semeia: The Bible and Feminist Hermeneutics*, 28 (1983): 3-28.

46. Paul Achtemeier, "Toward the Isolation of Pre-Markan Miracle Catena," *Journal of Biblical Literature* 89 (1970): 265-291 and "The Origin and Function of the Pre-Marcan Miracle Catena," *Journal of Biblical Literature* 91 (1972): 198-221.

47. Swidler, *Women in Judaism*, pp. 123-125.

48. Mark 5:32-34; 7:27-28; T. A. Burkill, "The Syrophoenician Woman. The Congruence of Mark 7:24-31," *Zeitschrift für die Neutestamentliche Wissenschaft* 52 (1966): 31.

49. Burkill, "Syrophoenician Woman," pp. 23-37. See also Erich Klosterman, *Das Markusevangelium* (Tübingen: Mohr, 1950), pp. 58-62; Bundy, *Jesus and the First Three Gospels: An Introduction to the Synoptic Tradition* (Cambridge: Harvard University Press, 1955), p. 278.

50. Ibid. Burkill's observations are astute. The writings of Mark do not anticipate a mission to the non-Jews, but give evidence that the present community is not totally Jewish. These stories serve as legends or etiologies about why certain people are now in the community and should be a vital part of the present gathering.

51. Some manuscripts add "when men rise from the dead" to the end of this verse. See Bruce M. Metzger, *A Textual Commentary on the Greek New Testament* (London: United Bible Societies, 1971), pp. 110-111. Some think that Jews believed that only the circumcised (and thus males) could make it to heaven. See James M. Robinson, Director. *The Nag-Hammadi Library in English* (New York: Harper and Row, 1977), p. 130. *The Gospel of Thomas* reads, "For every woman who will make herself male will enter the kingdom of Heaven."

52. Rachel Wahlberg suggests that the issue is over childbearing. See: *Jesus According to a Woman* (New York: Paulist Press, 1975), p. 64 and the *In-*

terpreter's Bible on this verse. 1951 ed.

53. Augustine. *The City of God*, 23:17; P. K. Jewett, *Man as Male and Female* (Grand Rapids: Eerdmans, 1978), p. 41; Rosemary Radford Ruether, "Misogynism and Virginal Feminism in the Fathers of the Church," in *Religion and Sexism*, ed. R. Radford Ruether (New York: Simon and Schuster, 1974), p. 160.

54. Swidler, *Woman in Judaism*, pp. 144-147; Roland Devaux, *Ancient Israel: Its Life and Institutions*, trans. John McHugh (New York: McGraw-Hill, 1961), pp. 24-33.

55. Evelyn and Frank Stagg, *Woman in the World of Jesus* (Philadelphia: Westminster, 1978), p. 138.

56. Kee, *Community of Mark*, p. 156.

57. Jewett, *Man as Male and Female*, p. 34.

58. In Genesis Rebekah seems to choose Isaac (Gen. 24:28-40). See also Exodus 20:17.

59. *Oxford Classical Dictionary*, 1970 ed., S. V. "Delphic Oracles," and W. C. Allen, "St. Mark XVI:8: 'They were Afraid': Why?" *Journal of Theological Studies* 47 (1946) says, "Their fear was not fright or terror but a solemn awe of human beings who felt they stood at the gate of heaven."

60. H. B. Swete, *The Gospel According to St. Mark* (London: Macmillan and Co., 1908), p. 34; A. M. Hunter, *The Gospel According to St. Luke* (London: SCM Press, 1948), p. 65.

61. Winsom Munro, "Woman Disciples in Mark," *Catholic Biblical Quarterly* 44 (1982): 225-241; See also T. E. Boomershine, "Mark 16:8 and the Apostolic Commission," *Journal of Biblical Literature* 100 (1981): 225-239.

62. Mark 4:41; 5:15; 6:50; 9:32; 11:18, etc. See also Luke 1:50; 18:2, 4; Acts 10:35; 1 Peter 2:17; Revelation 14:7; 19:5; and See Selvidge, "And Those Who Followed Feared."

63. *Phobos* ("fear"), *Theological Dictionary of the New Testament*, 1974 ed.

64. *Thambos* ("tremble"), *Theological Dictionary of the New Testament*, 1965 ed.

65. Irene Brennan, "Women in the Gospels," *New Blackfriars* 52 (1971), p. 299; see also Yershalmi Sanhedrin 3.9 in *The Babylonian Talmud*, ed. I. Epstein.

66. R. H. Smith, "New and Old in Mark 16:1-8." *Concordia Theological Monthly* 48 (1972): 518-527.

67. Burkill, "Syrophoenician Woman," p. 33.

68. Ibid., p. 35.

Chapter Two

1. Mark's gospel ends with only a hope, "He is going before you to Galilee; there you will see him, as he told you" (Mark 16:7). Jesus never returns. The people are left with their hopes for tomorrow as they journey to the north. Why Mark has ended the gospel in such a manner has been debated for centuries. I interpret the ending as positive. The women continue living their lives as they had in the past. They are successful. See the following for recent views on the meaning of the ending in Mark: *Oxford Classical Dictionary*, 1970 ed., S. V. "Delphic Oracles," W. C. Allen, "St. Mark XVI:8. 'They were afraid': Why?" *Journal of*

Theological Studies 47 (1946): 46-49 says, "Their fear was not fright or terror but a solemn awe of human beings who felt they stood at the gate of heaven. . . ." T. E. Boomershine, "Mark 16:8 and the Apostolic Commission," *Journal of Biblical Literature*, 100 (1981): 225-239. See his footnote no. 2 for a history of the interpretation of Mark's ending.

2. According to B. W. Bacon, *Studies in Matthew* (London: Constable, 1930), the gospel is structured into five blocks of teaching—a paradigm of the Torah. Jesus is viewed as the New Moses. He has authority over the Scriptures, "You have heard that it was said to the people long ago. . . . But I tell you . . ." (Matt. 5:21-22, NIV). Matthew also edits the miracle stories in order to show Jesus as being the one in power, in charge of the miracle. See: B. Bornkamm, B. Barth, and H. J. Held, *Tradition and Interpretation in Matthew* (Philadelphia: Westminster Press, 1963), pp. 215-219 and also J. D. Kingsbury, *Matthew: Structure, Christology, and Kingdom* (Philadelphia: Fortress Press, 1975).

3. Douglas R. A. Hare and Daniel J. Harrington, "Make Disciples of all Gentiles" (Matt. 28:19), *Catholic Biblical Quarterly* 31 (1975): 359-369.

4. For a discussion of the audience of Matthew see: B. H. Streeter, *The Four Gospels: A Study of Origins* (London: The Macmillan Co., 1924). See also Werner Georg Kümmel, *Introduction to the New Testament*, trans. H. C. Kee (New York: Abingdon Press, 1975), pp. 114-119.

5. Matthew omits the story about corban (Mark 7:10-13) and the widow's mite (Mark 12:41-44).

6. Matthew uses *lupētheis* ("sorry") in 14:9 and Mark uses *perilupos genomenos* ("exceedingly sorry") in 6:26 to describe her feelings.

7. Studies on the topic of divorce in the Synoptics is voluminous. Here is a list of recent English works that address the subject. Joseph A. Fitzmyer, *To Advance the Gospel* (New York: Crossroads, 1979), pp. 70-111; B. Byron, "The meaning of 'Except It Be for Fornication,' " *Australasian Catholic Record* 40 (1963): 90-95; J. Kodell, "The Celibacy Logion in Matthew 19:12," *Biblical Theology Bulletin* 8 (1978): 19-23; F. J, Moloney, "Matthew 19:3-12 and Celibacy. A Redactional and Form-Critical Study," *Journal of New Testament* 2 (1979): 46-50; Q. Quesnell, "Made Themselves Eunuchs for the Kingdom of Heaven, Matt. 19:12," *Catholic Biblical Quarterly* 30 (1968):335-358; L. Sabourin, "The Divorce Clauses (Matt. 5:32; 19:9)," *Biblical Theology Bulletin* 2 (1972):80-86; Augustine Stock, "Matthean Divorce Texts," *Biblical Theology Bulletin* 8 (1978): 24-33; T. L. Thompson, "A Catholic View on Divorce," *Journal of Ecumenical Studies* 6 (1969): 53-67; Bruce Vawter, "Divorce and the New Testament," *Catholic Biblical Quarterly* 39 (1977):528-542.

8. See *National Crime Survey*, Bureau of Justice Statistics, (1984); FBI, *Uniform Crime Reports*, (1982); William A. Stacey and Anson Shupe, *The Family Secret* (Boston: Beacon Press, 1983).

9. Fitzmyer, *To Advance the Gospel*, pp. 86f. discusses possible meanings for the "exception" clause in Matthew.

10. See Moloney, "Matthew 29:3-12 and Celibacy," pp. 19-23.

11. A. W. Argyle, "Wedding Customs at the Time of Jesus," *Expository Times* 86 (1975): 214-215.

12. K. P. Donfried, "The Allegory of the Ten Virgins (Matt. 25:1-13) as a Summary of Matthean Theology," *Journal of Biblical Literature* 93 (1974): 415-428.

13. Herman C. Waetjen, "The Genealogy as the Key to the Gospel According to Matthew, "*Journal of Biblical Literature* 95 (1976): 205-230; M. D. Johnson, *The Purpose of Biblical Genealogies with Special Reference to the Setting of the Genealogies of Jesus* (New York: Cambridge, 1969). For another opinion see James Lagrand, "How Was the Virgin Mary Like a Man?" *Novum Testamentum* 22 (1980): 97-107.

14. See Waetjen, "The Genealogy," pp. 105:230, and Johnson, *Purpose of the Biblical Genealogies*, p. 154.

15. Steven Bowman, "A New Look at Ruth," a paper delivered at the 1982 joint AAR/SBL in New York, sees Ruth as a very progressive and liberated woman. She is in charge of her life as well as her husband's. She chooses her next husband by having the audacity to sleep at his feet.

16. Johnson, *Purpose of Biblical Genealogies*, pp. 154ff.

17. The term means both male and female. It comes from the word *anēr* ("man") and *gunē* ("woman"). It speaks of a person that has personality characteristics that could be stereotypically labeled male and female. The term conjures up the idea of the best of both sexes.

18. Janice Capel Anderson, "Matthew: Gender and Reading," in *Semeia: The Bible and Feminist Hermeneutics*, 28 (1983): 7.

19. Herman Waetjen, *The Origin and Destiny of Humanness. An Interpretation of the Gospel of Matthew* (California: Omega Books, 1976), p. 198.

20. Some MSS. add *kai Iōsēph* ("and Joseph") to the text.

21. Harvey K. McArthur, "Son of Mary" *Novum Testamentum* 15(1973): 39-58.

22. Only men were required to keep the festival within Judaism. The sign of membership was "circumcision" which excludes women. Jewish men were encouraged not to talk with women in public. And women were required to cloister themselves from the public during their menstrual period. For a discussion of these issues see Leonard Swidler, *Woman in Judaism: The Status of Women in Formative Judaism* (New Jersey: The Scarecrow Press, 1976) and Roland DeVaux, *Ancient Israel: Its Life and Institutions*. trans. John McHugh (New York: McGraw Hill, 1961), pp. 24-33.

23. Swidler, *Woman in Judaism*, pp. 125-126.

24. Theodore J. Weeden, *Mark: Traditions in Conflict* (Philadelphia: Fortress Press, 1971), pp. 20-51, who explores the ineptness of the twelve.

25. R. Bultmann thinks the disciples were not the only ones to question Jesus. See *History of the Synoptic Tradition*, trans. John Marsh (New York: Harper and Row, 1963), p. 68.

26. For a discussion of women being alone with Jesus see W. D. Thompson, *Matthew's Advice to a Divided Community* (Rome: Biblical Institute Press, 1970), pp. 86-93.

27. *Krateō* ("to grasp"), *A Greek-English Lexicon of the New Testament and other Early Christian Literature*, 1979 ed.

28. R. A. Harrisville, "The Woman of Canaan: A Chapter in the History of

Exegesis," *Interpretation* 20 *(1966): 280, says Mark's description of the woman is political and Matthew's is religious. See also Kenzo Tagawa, "People and the Community in the Gospel of Matthew," New Testament Studies* 16 (1969): 149-162, who discusses the community's origins and socioreligious affiliations. Mark sets the scene at the border of Tyre (7:24)—*ta horia* ("border"). See also *horia* ("parts") in *A Greek Lexicon of the New Testament and other Early Christian Literature,* 1979 ed. Matthew says *ta merē* ("the parts") of Tyre and Sidon (15:26-27).

29. Harrisville, "Woman of Canaan," p. 276, says there is a harsh, biting quality in Matthew's account.

30. Bultmann, *History of the Synoptic Tradition,* p. 353 sees this phrase as a later edition. Harrisville, "Woman of Canaan," p. 283, understands it as her own view of herself. She thinks she should be treated like a dog.

31. Jack D. Kingsbury, *Matthew: Structure, Christology, Kingdom* (Philadelphia: Fortress Press, 1975), pp. 99-103; see also Harrisville, "Woman of Canaan," p. 278 for references and discussion of "Son of David."

32. Evelyn and Frank Stagg, *Woman in the World of Jesus,* p. 114. She is victorious and vindicated. See also Jerome H. Neyrey, "Decision Making in the Early Church. The Case of the Canaanite Woman (Matt. 15:21-28)," *Science et Esprit* 33 (1981): 373-378.

33. Elisabeth Schüssler Fiorenza was so impressed by this story that she entitled her award-winning book about women in the early church, *In Memory of Her* (New York: Crossroads, 1984).

34. *Kriein* ("anoint") is used in 1 Sam. 9:16; 15:1; 16:3, 12; 2 Sam. 5:3; 12:7; 19:10; 1 Kings 1:34; 2 Kings 9:12; 2 Chron. 23:11, etc. See *aleiphō* ("anoint") in *The Interpreter's Dictionary of the Bible,* 1962 ed. Elizabeth E. Pratt, "The Ministry of Mary of Bethany," *Theology Today* 34 (1977): 29-39, compares all four accounts of the anointing.

35. Jealousy on the part of the disciples is mirrored in some of the Gnostic writings. See E. Pagels, *The Gnostic Gospels* (New York: Random House, 1979), pp. 48-69.

36. Ben Witherington III, "On the Road with Mary Magdalene, Joanna, Susanna, and other Disciples, Luke 8:1-3," *Zeitschrift für die Neutestamentliche Wissenschaft* 70 (1979): 243-248, and M. J. Selvidge, "The Leadership of Women in the Marcan Community," *Listening* 15 (1980): 250-256.

37. Jack D. Kingsbury, "The Verb *Akoloutheō* ["to follow"] as an Index of Matthew's View of his Community," *Journal of Biblical Literature* 98 (1978): 61-73.

38. *Akoloutheō* ("to follow") in *The Theological Dictionary of the New Testament,* ed. 1964.

39. Ibid.

40. Ibid., p. 214.

41. M. J. Selvidge (Schierling), "Reflections on Serving: Mark and Woman," *Explorations: A Journal for Adventurous Thought* (Dayton, Ohio) 1 (1982): 23-32.

42. Mark uses the imperfect active *diēkonoun* ("served") and *ēkolouthoun*

("followed") in 15:41 and Matthew accomplishes the same idea by using an aorist, *ēkolouthēsan* ("followed") and a present participle *diakonousai* ("while serving") in 27:55. Matthew may be suggesting that their following ceases at Jesus' death but their serving did not. Mark sees their activities of following and serving as a past event that continues into the future. See: F. Blass and A. De-Brunner, *A Greek Grammar of the New Testament and other Early Christian Literature* (Chicago: University of Chicago Press, 1961), p. 171, no. 332, and p. 169, no. 327.

43. *Diakoneō* ("to serve") in *The Theological Dictionary of the New Testament*, 1964 ed.

44. Ibid.

45. Ibid., p. 85.

46. The word *onar* is not used in the LXX. See *onar* ("dream") in *The Theological Dictionary of the New Testament*, 1967 ed.

47. T. E. Boomershine, "Mark 16:8 and the Apostolic Commission," *Journal of Biblical Literature* 100 (1981): 225-239. See footnote no. 2 for the history of interpretation of Mark's ending.

48. *Proskuneō* ("worship") in *The Greek-English Dictionary of the New Testament and Other Early Christian Literature*, 1979 ed.

Chapter Three

1. See my article, "Violence in Matthew: A Seminal Investigative Study" in *Proceedings of the Eastern Great Lakes Biblical Conference, 1984*. Luke often uses "Q." Eighty percent of those traditions contain violent or abusive language. In a study of 64 violent words found in Luke, 29 of these words appear more often in Luke than in the other Synoptics. This may suggest that Luke is more violent. Yet after a careful study it may also be noted that of these 29, 14 are only used by Luke. Usually Luke replaces words used by Mark or Q with synonyms.

2. Werner Georg Kümmel, *An Introduction to the New Testament* (New York: Abingdon Press, 1973), pp. 98-101.

3. Recent books center on Luke's political themes. See, for instance, Richard J. Cassidy, *Jesus, Politics, and Society: A Study of Luke's Gospel* (New York: Orbis Books, 1980); and Richard J. Cassidy and Philip J. Scharper (eds.), *Political Issues in Luke-Acts* (New York: Orbis Books, 1983); Walter E. Pilgrim, *Good News to the Poor: Wealth and Poverty in Luke-Acts* (Minneapolis: Augsburg, 1981).

4. Robin Scroggs, "The Earliest Christian Communities as Sectarian Movements" in *Christianity, Judaism, and other Greco-Roman Cults. Studies for Morton Smith at 60*. 2 vols., ed. Jacob Neusner (Leiden: E. J. Brill, 1975) Vol. II: 1-23. John G. Gager, *Kingdom and Community: The Social World of Early Christianity* (New Jersey: Prentice Hall, 1975).

5. According to most scholars, Luke is primarily writing to a Gentile audience. For a discussion of the community of Luke, read Joseph A. Fitzmyer, *The Gospel According to Luke. I-IX, The Anchor Bible* (New York: Doubleday and Company, 1981), pp. 53-62.

6. Ibid., pp. 107-108.

7. Much debate still surrounds the origin of Luke's special material. Did the writer use other sources or did the writer create narratives? See Paul S. Minear, "Luke's use of the Birth Stories," in *Studies in Luke-Acts*, eds. L. E. Keck and J. L. Martyn (New York: Abingdon Press, 1966), pp. 111-130.

8. Raymond E. Brown, *The Birth of the Messiah: A Commentary on the Infancy Narratives in Matthew and Luke* (New York: Image Books, 1979), pp. 292-301.

9. This is according to G. Graystone, "The Mother of Jesus in the Synoptics," in the *New Catholic Commentary on Holy Scripture*, ed. R. Fuller (London: Nelson, 1969), pp. 661ff. E. H. Maly, "Women and the Gospel of Luke," *Biblical Theology Bulletin* 10 (1980), 99-104, sees a "new way of interpreting" society in the woman stories in Luke.

10. J. A. Grassi, "Luke the Theologian of Grace, and Mary, the Mother of Jesus," *Bible Today* 51 (1970) 148-154.

11. This is the only time that Luke uses the feminine form of *servant*. Servants are mentioned elsewhere but none are called "blessed."

12. Elisabeth Schüssler Fiorenza, *In Memory of Her: A Feminist Theological Reconstruction of Christian Origins* (New York: Crossroads, 1983), p. 142.

13. Hans Conzelmann, *The Theology of St. Luke*, Trans. G. Buswell (Philadelphia: Fortress Press, 1961), p. 172.

14. Brown, *Birth of the Messiah*, p. 297; Grassi, "Luke the Theologian," p. 152; I. Howard Marshall, *The Gospel of Luke: A Commentary on the Greek Text* in The New International Greek Testament Commentary series. Grand Rapids: William B. Eerdmans, 1978, pp. 45-165.

15. M. E. Isaacs, "Mary in the Lucan Infancy Narrative," *Way Supplement* 25 (1975):87-88.

16. Brown, *Birth of the Messiah*, p. 297.

17. Isaacs, "Mary in the Lucan," pp. 87-88.

18. See similar stories in Judges 5:24; Judith 13:18; Deuteronomy 7:12-14.

19. Elizabeth is mentioned at the beginning of some ancient manuscripts.

20. Fitzmyer, *The Gospel According to Luke*, p. 424.

21. Marla J. (Schierling) Selvidge, *Luke the Feminist: A Study of Luke's Presentation of the Women in Luke-Acts* (Thesis: 1973), p. 38.

22. See Leviticus 12—15 and my dissertation *Woman, Cult, and Miracle Recital: Mark 5:24-34* (St. Louis University: 1980), pp. 126-142.

23. The word used here is *esplanchnisthē* ("his heart [or intestines] went out to her").

24. *Klaiō* ("to weep") is found in Matthew 2:18; 26:75; Mark 5:38, 39; 14:72; Luke 6:21, 25; 7:13, 32, 38; 8:52; 19:41; 23:28.

25. Theodore Hertzl is the well-known Jewish leader who began the Zionist movement to Israel in the nineteenth century. In 1948 Israel became an independent country.

26. Calvin Coolidge (1872-1933) was the thirtieth president of the United States.

27. Josephus, *The Jewish Wars*, Loeb Classical Library, p. 447.

28. See Walter Bauer, et. al., *A Greek-English Lexicon of the New Testament*

and Other Early Christian Literature. Second Edition (Chicago: University of Chicago, 1979), *asēr* ("Asher"), p. 115.

29. William Manson, *The Gospel of Luke* (London: Hodder and Stoughton, 1945), p. 21, says that Simeon was a "type of those Jewish saints whose eyes were continually turning towards the Messianic dawn."

30. R. L. Hemenay, "The Place of Mary in Luke: A Look at Modern Biblical Criticism," *American Ecclesiastic Review* 168 (1974), p. 300. He gives several interpretations of the phrase "piercing the heart." He says it could be a doubtful, a hesitating, or a thoughtful person.

31. Gerhard Friedrich, *Theological Dictionary of the New Testament* Vol. VI (Grand Rapids: Eerdmans, 1968), *prophētēs* ("prophetess"), p. 829.

32. A. T. Varela, "Luke 2:36-37: Is Anna's Age What Is Really in Focus?" *Bible Translation* 27 (1976), p. 446. He suggests that her life was above average and hints that her life as a widow was even better than that of a wife.

33. See Deuteronomy 25:5 and Genesis 38:8.

34. According to Luke, John the Baptist had angels (or messengers) and he himself functioned as an angel or a messenger (see Luke 7:24). Angels are called holy (Luke 9:26), they name children (Luke 2:21), deliver messages (Luke 9:52), and sing out their hearts (Luke 2:13). Some are even called "angels of God" (Luke 12:8, 9).

35. Read Rosemary Radford Ruether, "Misogynism and Virginal Feminism in the Fathers of the Church," in *Religion and Sexism: Images of Woman in the Jewish and Christian Traditions*, ed. R. R. Ruether (New York: Simon and Schuster, 1974), pp. 117-149, and Ruether's, "Motherearth and the Megamachine," in *Womanspirit Rising: A Feminist Reader in Religion*," eds. Carol P. Christ and Judith Plaskow (New York: Harper and Row, 1979), pp. 43-52.

36. Listen to the song, "I Don't Know How to Love Him." Words and music by Tim Rice and Andrew Lloyd Weber in the rock opera *Jesus Christ Superstar* (New York: Decca Records, N.Dak.).

37. Elaine Pagels, *The Gnostic Gospels* (New York: Vintage Books, 1981), pp. 77, 79.

38. Irene Brennan, "Women in the Gospels," *New Blackfriars* 52 (1971):295.

39. Many commentaries omit this verse altogether from their comments. They do not seem to understand it. It does not fit into their theology.

40. These quotations betray a time that is similar to the fall of Jerusalem as told by Josephus, *The Jewish Wars*, Loeb Classical Library.

41. Many places have been suggested (i.e., Caesarea, Achaia, Syria). See any introduction to the New Testament or the introduction of any commentary on Luke.

42. Fiorenza, *In Memory of Her*, p. 146.

43. Varela, "Is Anna's Age . . .," p. 446, indicates that the single woman is the wiser of the two.

44. Fiorenza, *In Memory of Her*, pp. 145-146. In Luke's revision of Mark 10:29b (Luke 18:29b) *wife* is added. Based upon Mark's original exclusion she concludes that the "Jesus movement was a charismatic movement of wandering men, sons, and husbands. . . ."

45. According to Mary Rose D'Angelo, "Women and the Earliest Church: Reflecting on the Problematique of Christ and Culture," in *Woman Priests: A Catholic Commentary on the Vatican Declaration*, eds. Leonard Swidler and Arlene Swidler (New York: Paulist Press, 1977), p. 280, "Wealthy and prominent Gentile women, including the Emperor's daughter, appear throughout the Talmud and Midrashim as inquirers and patrons of Rabbis (e.g., B.San. 39a)." Josephus frequently refers to the support of wealthy women proselytes and "God-fearers"; especially notable in the case of Helena, Queen of Adiabene. See *Jewish Antiquities*. The Loeb Classical Library, XX, ii.

46. See Fiorenza, *In Memory of Her*, pp. 139-140.

47. J. Massyngberde Ford, "Woman Leaders in the New Testament," in *Women Priests: A Catholic Commentary*, p. 133.

48. D'Angelo, "Women and Earliest Church," pp. 191-200.

49. Elizabeth Moltmann-Wendel, *The Women around Jesus* (New York: Crossroads, 1982), pp. 138, 141.

50. Ben Witherington III, "On the Road with Mary Magdalene, Joanna, Susanna, and other Disciples—Luke 8:1-3," *Zeitschrift für die Neutestamentliche Wissenschaft* 70 (1979): 247. See also Marshall, *Commentary on Luke*, p. 315.

51. Marshall, *The Gospel of Luke*, pp. 314-317.

52. There are two possible readings for this text, either "them" or "him." Joseph Fitzmyer, *Commentary on Luke,* p. 698, says, "Some Greek mss. of the Hesychian tradition (A), the Lake family of minuscules, and some OL texts along with Vg^cl read the sg. *autō* 'him.' "

53. According to M. Adinolfi, "Les Discepole di Gesu," *Bibbia e Oriente* (Bornato) 16 (1947):10-12 the verb "to follow" indicates a permanent adhesion.

54. See the discussion of this account in the chapter on Mark.

55. See Paul K. Jewett, *Man as Male and Female: A Study in Sexual Relationships from a Theological Point of View* (Grand Rapids: Eerdmans, 1975), p. 99.

56. Leonard Swidler, *Woman in Judaism: The Status of Women in Formative Judaism* (New Jersey: The Scarecrow Press, 1976), pp. 114-125.

57. Richard J. Dillon, *From Eye-Witness to Ministers of the Word* (Rome: Biblical Institute Press, 1978), p. 239.

58. Read the New Testament book, Acts of the Apostles. Note that most of the Christian gatherings are in homes.

59. See Floyd V. Filson, "The Significance of the Early House Churches," *Journal of Biblical Literature* 58 (1939):105-112.

60. See James 2:2 and Bauer, *A Greek-English Lexicon, sunagōgē* ("synagogue"), p. 783. G. Friedrich, *Theological Dictionary of the New Testament* (Grand Rapids: Eerdmans, 1971) *sunagōgē* ("synagogue"), pp. 815, 828, 838ff. He has an excellent discussion on the archaeology and use of the term as a word for congregation during the post-apostolic period of the church.

61. Filson, "Early House Churches," p. 112.

62. Schüssler-Fiorenza, *In Memory of Her*, p. 168.

63. D. W. Riddle, "Early Christian Hospitality. A Factor in the Gospel

Transmission," *Journal of Biblical Literature* 57 (1938): 143.

64. G. H. P. Thompson, *The Gospel According to Luke* (Oxford: The Clarendon Press, 1972), p. 162, says, "Martha has been occupied preparing a varied menu of dishes, but Mary has chosen the one good part and really adequate dish: listening to Jesus."

65. This is contrary to E. Moltmann-Wendel, *The Women Around Jesus* (New York: Crossroads, 1982), p. 21. Moltmann-Wendel says, "If Mary is the embodiment of reflective contemplative Christianity, Martha is the embodiment of active Christianity."

66. See Rachel Wahlberg, *Jesus According to Women* (New York: Paulist Press, 1975), p. 77. Wahlberg assumes that Martha is in the kitchen. "Martha knows she is right, managing the work in the kitchen. She knows what should be served and how to go about preparing it." See also Fiorenza, *In Memory of Her*, p. 165. Her footnote 11 on page 200 discusses E. Laland, "Die Martha-Maria Perikope in Lukas 10, 38-42," *Studia Theologia* 13 (1959): 70-85. Laland thinks that the early church wanted to keep women to "practical serving functions." In *Women Around Jesus*, pp. 28-50, Moltmann-Wendel point out that Martha was considered in the middle ages a vanquisher of dragons.

67. R. Holst, "The One Anointing of Jesus," *Journal of Biblical Literature* 95 (1976): 435-446. See his footnote 2 for a discussion of those who see two different events or traditions.

68. See Fiorenza, *In Memory of Her*, p. 128.

69. J. D. M. Derrett, *Law in the New Testament* (London: Daron, Logmann, and Todd, 1970), pp. 266-278; Marshall, *Commentary on Luke*, pp. 304ff., lists a variety of writers who interpret this woman to be either an adulteress or a prostitute.

70. Jewett, *Man as Male and Female*, p. 100.

71. Schüssler-Fiorenza, *In Memory of Her*, p. 129, says she is a prostitute.

72. Ibid., p. 128.

73. Q. Quesnell, "The Women at Luke's Supper," in *Political Issues in Luke-Acts*, ed. Richard J. Cassidy and Philip J. Sharper (New York: Orbis, 1983), pp. 59-71; see also Dillon, *From Eyewitness to Ministers of the Word*, p. 11.

74. Wahlberg, *Jesus according to Woman*, p. 51.

75. Ibid., p. 56.

76. M. C. Detrick, "Jesus and Woman," *Brethren Life and Thought* 22 (1977): 157.

77. Mary Daly, *Gyn/Ecology: The Metaethics of Radical Feminism* (Boston: Beacon Press, 1978), pp. 380-384. She creates a brilliant journey for woman beyond patriarchy. Her language opens a passageway to view the world differently. In breaking open this new world, she herself does not avoid violent or abusive language. See also Schüssler-Fiorenza, *In Memory of Her*, pp. 104-140ff.

78. H. Flender, *St. Luke: Theologian of Redemptive History* (Philadelphia: Fortress Press, 1967), p. 51.

79. Constance Parvey, "The Theology and Leadership of Women in the New Testament," in *Religion and Sexism: Images of Women in the Jewish and Chris-*

tian Traditions, ed. Rosemary Radford Ruether (New York: Simon and Schuster, 1974), pp. 139ff.

80. For research in this area see Joachim Jeremias, *The Parables of Jesus* (New York: Charles Scribners Sons, 1955), pp. 70-74; N. M. Flanagan, "The Position of Women in the Writings of Luke," *Marianum* 40 (1978):288-304; and Leonard Swidler, *Biblical Affirmations* of Woman (Philadelphia: Westminster Press, 1979), pp. 165-172.

81. Jess Stein, ed. *The Random House Dictionary* (New York: Ballantine Books, 1980), p. 363.

82. Gerhard Friedrich, *Theological Dictionary of the New Testament*, Vol. IX (Grand Rapids: Eerdmans, 1974), *Phileō* ("love"), pp. 146-149.

83. The feminine word for friend—*philas*—is used in Luke 15:6.

84. *Heteros* ("other") is used 9 times by Matthew, 1 time by Mark, and 33 times by Luke. *Allēlous* ("one another") is used 3 times by Matthew, 5 times by Mark, and 11 times by Luke.

85. Schüssler-Fiorenza, *In Memory of Her*, p. 49.

86. Ibid.

87. Dillon, *From Eyewitness to Ministers of the Word*, p. 56.

88. For the Jewish attitude toward women as witnesses, see: J. B. Segal, "The Jewish Attitude Towards Women," *Journal of Jewish Studies* 30 (1979):121-137.

89. Swidler, *Women in Judaism*, pp. 115-117.

90. The word *apostle* may be a later addition. Dillon, *From Eyewitness to Ministers of the Word*, pp. 61-62, has an extensive discussion of the manuscript evidence and reasons for the inclusion of this verse.

91. Ibid., p. 58.

92. Ibid., p. 67; see also Luke 8:25 and Mark 4:41.

93. Ibid., p. 52.

Chapter Four

1. Ann Thatcher, "The World of Women," in *Women's Spirit Bonding*, eds. Janet Kalven and Mary I. Buckley (New York: The Pilgrim Press, 1984), p. 151.

2. Rubem Alves, *What Is Religion?* (New York: Orbis Books, 1984), p. 8.

3. Sheila Collins, "Reflections on the Meaning of Herstory," in *Womanspirit Rising: A Feminist Reader in Religion*, eds. Carol P. Christ and Judith Plaskow (New York: Harper and Row, 1979), p. 68.

4. Phyllis Trible, "The Opportunity of Loneliness," in *Women and the Word-Sermons*, ed. Helen Gray Crotwell (Phil.: Fortress Press, 1978).

5. James Kavanaugh, *There Are Men Too Gentle to Live Among Wolves* (New York: E. P. Dutton, 1970). See the opening unnumbered pages.

Suggested Reading

Women and the Synoptics

Elisabeth Schüssler Fiorenza. *In Memory of Her* (New York: Crossroads, 1984.

Paul K. Jewett. *Man as Male and Female* (Grand Rapids: Eerdmans, 1978).

Janice Nunnally-Cox. *Foremothers: Women of the Bible* (New York: Seabury Press, 1981).

Rosemary Radford Ruether, ed. *Religion and Sexism: Images of Women in the Jewish and Christian Traditions* (New York: Simon and Schuster, 1974).

Evelyn and Frank Stagg. *Woman in the World of Jesus* (Philadelphia: Westminster, 1978).

Rachel Wahlberg, *Jesus According to Woman* (New York: Paulist Press, 1975).

Elizabeth Moltmann-Wendel, *The Women Around Jesus* (New York: Crossroads, 1982).

Women: Ancient and Modern

J. P. V. Balsdon. *Roman Women: Their History and Habits* (London: Badley Head, 1962).

Carol P. Christ and Judith Plaskow, eds. *Woman-spirit Rising: A Feminist Reader in Religion* (New York: Harper and Row, 1979).

Elaine Pagels. *The Gnostic Gospels* (New York: Random House, 1979).

S. B. Pomeroy. *Goddesses, Whores, Wives, and Slaves: Women in Classical Antiquity.* (New York: Schocken Press, 1975).

Letha Scanzoni and Nancy Hardesty. *All We're Meant to Be: A Biblical Approach to Women's Liberation* (Texas: Word Books, 1975).

Leonard Swidler. *Women in Judaism: The Status of Women in Formative Judaism* (New Jersey: Scarecrow Press, 1976).

New Testament: Introduction and Methodology

J. Harold Greenlee. *Scribes, Scrolls, and Scripture: A Student's Guide to New Testament Criticism* (Grand Rapids: William B. Eerdman's, 1985).

John H. Hayes and Carl R. Holladay. *Biblical Exegesis: A Beginner's Handbook* (Atlanta: John Knox Press, 1982).

Norman Perrin. *What Is Redaction Criticism?* (Philadelphia: Fortress Press, 1969).

Norman Perrin and Dennis Duling. *The New Testament: An Introduction: Proclamation and Parenesis, Myth, and History.* Second Edition (New York: Harcourt, Brace, Jovanovich, Inc., 1982).

The Synoptics

The Synoptic Problem
Rudolph Bultmann. *History of the Synoptic Tradition.* Trans. J.

Marsh (New York: Harper and Row, 1963).

Ron Cameron, ed. *The Other Gospels: Non-Canonical Texts* (Philadelphia: Westminster, 1982).

B. H. Streeter. *The Four Gospels: A Study of Origins* (London: The Macmillan Co., 1930).

The Gospel of Mark

Sean P. Kealy, Mark's Gospel. *A History of Its Interpretation* (New York: Paulist Press, 1982).

Howard C. Kee. *Community of the New Age: Studies in Mark's Gospel* (Philadelphia: The Westminster Press, 1977).

David Rhoades and Donald Michie, *Mark as Story: An Introduction to the Narrative of a Gospel* (Philadelphia: Fortress Press: 1982).

Theodore J. Weeden. *Mark: Traditions in Conflict* (Philadelphia: Fortress Press, 1971).

The Gospel of Matthew

O. Lamar Cope. *Matthew: A Scribe Trained for the Kingdom of Heaven* (Washington: Catholic Biblical Association, 1976).

Jack D. Kingsbury. *Matthew: Structure, Christology, Kingdom* (Philadelphia: Fortress Press, 1975).

Herman Waetjen. *The Origin and Destiny of Humanness: An Interpretation of the Gospel of Matthew* (California: Omega Books, 1976).

The Gospel of Luke

Raymond E. Brown. *The Birth of the Messiah: A Commentary on the Infancy Narratives in Matthew and Luke* (New York: Image Books, 1979).

Richard J. Cassidy. *Jesus, Politics, and Society: A Study of Luke's Gospel* (New York: Orbis Books, 1980).

Hans Conzelmann, *The Theology of St. Luke*. Trans. G. Buswell (Philadelphia: Fortress Press, 1961).

History and Social Climate
During New Testament Times

John G. Gager. *The Social World of Early Christianity* (New Jersey: Prentice Hall, 1975).

Madeleine S. and J. Lane Miller. *Harper's Encyclopedia of Bible Life* (New York: Harper and Row, 1978).

Solomon Zeitlin. *The Rise and Fall of the Judean State* 3 vols. (Philadelphia: The Jewish Publication Society of America, 1978).

Index of Scriptures

The Author

An avid writer and lecturer, Dr. Marla Selvidge has spent over twenty years researching and writing about biblical texts. Her academic career has brought her into associations with Mennonites, Baptists, Roman Catholics, Lutherans, Methodists, and a variety of other religious groups, including Reform and Conservative Synagogues.

Selvidge earned her Ph.D. in biblical languages and literature from Saint Louis University and her Master's in New Testament from Wheaton College. Following her work at St. Louis University she accepted several academic and research positions, including appointments at the University of Dayton and Carthage College. She is currently assistant professor of religion at Converse College in Spartanburg, South Carolina.

Originally from Roseville, Michigan, Selvidge now lives with her husband, Thomas Hemling, an organic chemist, in Cowpens, South Carolina.